RD029364 Dxv

D1337984

Contents

List of Illustrations

Tyne Cot cemetery in 1919: the largest British war cemetery in the world. (IWM)

King George V presenting widows with their husbands' medals at Buckingham Palace. (IWM)

1920 British Legion pilgrimage to Vimy Ridge. Mothers and widows are buying wreaths for their son's or husband's grave at the cemetery. (IWM)

May 1919: Sister Maycock writing her address for a patient at Queen Mary's Hospital in Southend, just before it closed down. (Getty Images)

January 1919: Mutinous soldiers demonstrating peacefully against being sent to Russia. There were further mutinies by British troops in Russia. (Getty Images)

A year after the end of the war: a destitute family in Fleet Street, London. (Getty Images)

The body of the Unknown Warrior has been selected and is, with dignity, beginning his last journey. (IWM)

November 1920: The coffin of the Unknown Warrior is carried from the Citadel in Boulogne, on its way to his final resting place in Westminster Abbey. (Getty Images)

11 November 1920: The unveiling of the Cenotaph by King George V in Whitehall. On the same day the Unknown Warrior was buried. (IWM)

Acknowledgements

At my publishers, Weidenfeld and Nicolson, I would like to thank Ian Drury, the former Publishing Director for his inspired idea for the book and Keith Lowe for his editorial skills, his support and tenacity.

In the research for this book Samantha Crew spent countless hours at the Imperial War Museum typing up taped interviews and I thank her. Throughout the writing of this book I have had the great fortune to have Vicky Thomas who orchestrated so sensitively and accurately all the taped and transcribed interviews, for which I am profoundly grateful.

Within the Imperial War Museum I am indebted to Margaret Brooks, the Keeper of the Sound Archive; and to Peter Hart, the Museum's distinguished oral historian, for his advice and support throughout this book. The remarkable work of the Sound Archive has no parallel in this country, and future oral historians will benefit from the thousands of hours that its staff have recorded of servicemen and women involved in all the wars since the Great War. See the following page for a full list of the interviews used in this book. I am also most grateful to Chris Sheppard and Karen Mee of the Special Collections at the University of Leeds.

I would like to particularly thank the historian Lyn Macdonald for her permission to use several extracts from her excellent book on the Great War, *Ordeal by Fire*.

I want to thank my brother Adrian, an expert on the British Army, who always came up with the correct title for each regiment, many of whom are now lost in the fog of history.

Throughout the writing of this book I have the support of my dear friends Sir Martin and Lady Gilbert, Don and Liz McClen, David and Annie Rickards, Susan Jeffreys and Deborah Moggach.

Ruth Cowen has given me sound advice, much humour and affection. Her sensitivity and understanding has enriched this book and I profoundly thank her.

My final thanks go to Lucia Corti for her beauty and her love.

IWM Sound Archive Interviews:
32 Wilson
36 Thorpe
42 Martin
46 Grover
95 Benham
316 Woolley
330 Johnson
332 Ounsworth
377 Limerick
486 Wilkinson
507 Allwood
508 Evans
510 Wright
515 Edgley
559 Esler
737 Dixon
9279 Steward
9434 Collins
9926 Jones
9987 Bashford
10441 Grover
13731 Farr

Author's Preface

In 2005 I interviewed the last twenty-one veterans of the Great War for my book, *Last Post: The Final Words from our Soldiers of the Great War*. Each one was more than hundred years old, and all had vivid stories to tell of their experiences of the war. With the deaths of Henry Allingham and Harry Patch this year, there are now in Britain no living witnesses to the great campaigns, and their testimonies have passed into history.

Most oral histories of the Great War – my own included – have naturally concentrated on serving soldiers, and concluded at the end of the conflict. This time I wanted to shift the focus away from an exclusively military approach, and examine the immediate aftermath of the bloodiest conflict of modern times. It has become axiomatic to talk about the disappointment of the demobbed soldier, returning to a homeland that he had been assured would be fit for heroes, only to find unemployment, austerity and indifference.

What did the returning veterans really find at home? How did the shellshocked, the blind and the amputees manage to find a place in a society that the war had changed beyond all recognition? And what of those who had stayed at home – the conscientious objectors, the army of young widows, the spinsters without hope of a husband, the mothers who had sacrificed their sons. In this collection of testimonies all these people, and many more, tell their stories, and not all are what you might expect. From the grimmest of circumstances people did find the strength to rebuild their homes, their families and their working lives, with a tenacity, a determination and clear sense of purpose that only survivors of such a traumatic experience could have had.

Their accounts have been gathered principally from the archives of the Imperial War Museum, the Liddle Collection and contemporary news sources, and it has been a great privilege to hear such extraordinary tales of everyday optimism, stoicism and determination in the face of supreme difficulties. These are the words of real men and women: I have been but a catalyst.

Max Arthur
London
August 2009

CHAPTER I

The Armistice at the Front

As the last seconds of the war ticked away on the Western Front, some troops seized the opportunity to loose off their final rounds. Others, unable to believe that the hostilities of over four years were really about to end, sat quietly and waited. At last, over the devastation of the battlefields, the guns were silent.

Major Keith
Australian Expeditionary Force

At eleven o'clock on the 11th November I was sitting in a room in the Brewer's House at Le Cateau, which had been Sir John French's headquarters at the time of the Battle of Mons. I was sitting at a table with a major in the Scots Greys who had a large, old-fashioned hunting watch which he put on the table and watched the minutes ticking away. When eleven o'clock came, he shut his watch up and said, 'I wonder what we are all going to do next!' That was very much the feeling of everyone. What was one going to do next? To some of us it was the end of four years. For many of us it was practically the only life we had known. We had started so young.

Nearby there was a German machine-gun unit giving our troops a lot of trouble. They kept on firing until practically eleven o'clock. At precisely eleven o'clock, an officer stepped out of their position, stood up, lifted his helmet and bowed to us. He then fell in all his men in the front of the trench and marched them off. I always thought that was a wonderful display of confidence in British chivalry, because the temptation to fire on them must have been very great.

Marine Hubert Trotman
Royal Marine Light Infantry

We were still fighting hard and losing men. We knew nothing of the proposed Armistice – we didn't know until a quarter to ten on that day. As we advanced on the village of Guiry, a runner came up and told us that the Armistice would be signed at eleven o'clock that day, the 11th November. That was the first we knew of it.

We were lined up on a railway bank – the same railway bank that the Manchesters had lined up on in 1914. They had fought at the battle of Mons in August that year. Some of us went down to a wood in a little valley and found the skeletons of some of the Manchesters, still lying there – lying there with their boots on, very still, no helmets, no rusty rifles or equipment ... just their boots.

Corporal Thomas Grady
305th Machine Gun Battalion, Australian Expeditionary Force
(from his diary)

Stood by all night and it was a hot place. One of my guns was knocked out of action by shrapnel and I found one of the new men – Jones – dead in his dugout. Cold and raining. A runner came in at 10.30 with order to cease firing at 11 a.m. Firing continued and we stood by. The 306th Machine Gun Company on my right lost twelve men at 10.55 when a high explosive shell landed in their position. I reported Jones's death and marked his grave. The captain conducted a prayer and cried like a baby.

Anton Lang
2nd Bavarian Foot Artillery Regiment, Imperial German Army

The battle raged until exactly 11 a.m. and all of a sudden a 'big freeze' set in. One had a feeling it was a dream and unbelievable. The sudden stillness was interrupted by a single heavy shell, which exploded on a trail near our battery among a platoon of infantry and killed four and wounded about a dozen. Having seen so many tragedies this made us sad and mad. Some joker on the other side probably wanted to fire the 'last' shot.

Corporal Charles Templar
13th Battalion, Gloucestershire Regiment

Prior to the Armistice I really had no intimation that the war was going to end right when it did. Maybe there was a feeling that it was not going to carry on much longer, but I was at home on leave from 2 to 12 October. While I was at home I felt that perhaps I stood a chance of surviving – which is why I decided to propose to Daisy.

At home, my mother told me that my godfather was very ill in hospital with cancer – so I went to see him. I walked into his room, and the first thing he said to me was, 'Charles, don't go getting yourself killed now. The war won't last much longer and the country will need young men like you.' That was his view – and he was the one that was putting money in the bank for me and his wife while I was in the army.

Sergeant Arthur Allwood

7th Battalion, King's Own Shropshire Light Infantry

On the night of the 10th November, Colonel Burn called all officers to Battalion HQ and told us we were moving the next morning to relieve the Guards. At daybreak we marched away, but at 8 a.m. we heard to our relief that the Guards had taken Mauberge, and we would not be in action again that night. Then Colonel Burn read this dispatch to us SNCOs and officers about the end of hostilities. It said that there was to be no intercourse with the enemy – no Germans were to be allowed to enter our lines – and any doing so would be taken prisoner. The Colonel told us to break the news to the men as quietly as possible. I went back to A Company and simply said, 'It's all over, boys!' and they looked at me as if stunned. I don't think they believed it, then someone came along to verify it – and still they wouldn't take it in.

Once they realized, their first reaction was to ask how soon they could write to the people back home to let them know that they'd survived – and that's how I felt too. Then they asked the padre to hold a service as soon as we arrived back at our overnight billets.

Private Frank Dunk

7th Battalion, The Queen's Own (Royal West Kent Regiment)

On 10 November, my gun team came to a farm on the road towards the Belgian village of Sevry and we knocked on the front door. A woman opened it and was very surprised to see us. She put her fingers to her lips and, pointing inside, said, 'Boche!' When we went in the Germans left by the back door, leaving their breakfast behind them on the table – a black loaf, one tin of fat pork, and a dixie of coffee made with burnt wheat. We shared it between us, then went on our way.

We reached a crossroads half a mile nearer the village, and found that it had been tunnelled ready to blow up, so we took up positions some fifty yards back. We had been there for about an hour when a German patrol, nine in all, arrived – intending to blow the crossroads up. I shouted, 'Eh up!' and let fly with one pannier of bullets into the whole patrol. They ran in all directions, dropping the sticks of explosives.

In the afternoon, we were relieved by a battalion of the Manchester Regiment. We went back to Solre le Chateau and we were billeted for the night in a German bread store, where we had to sleep on stacks of black bread with rats running all over the place. The next morning we got up to see our officer coming down the street in his shirt and braces with a barrel of beer on a big French wheelbarrow. He came into the billet and said, 'Come on lads, the war will be over at eleven o'clock.' When the French folks heard, out came the flags and wine, beer – all sorts, and everybody got totally pickled.

Second Lieutenant Clifford Carter
2nd York and Lancaster Regiment

I had just marched my platoon to 'Baths', and was wandering aimlessly about the roads, waiting till they had finished, when I saw a signaller leap out of his billet and fix a notice to the wall outside: 'Hostilities will cease at 11.00 today'. It was one of the pleasantest duties of my army life to return to the baths and report the news to the men – adding that they would not have to return to the Front that night as had been expected.

It is quite impossible to describe the feeling of relief. Only those who were there could appreciate it fully.

Colonel W N Nicholson
The Suffolk Regiment

A German machine-gun remained in action the whole morning opposite our lines. Just before 11 a.m., a thousand rounds were fired from it in a practically ceaseless burst.

At 11 a.m. there came great cheering from the German lines and the village church bells rang. But on our side there were only a few shouts. I had heard more for a rum ration. The match was over – it had been a damned bad game.

Lieutenant-Colonel Rowland Fielding
6th Connaught Rangers

Yesterday we were to have pushed on and captured another town – Ath – which would have been a bloodless victory, since the enemy was retreating so fast that it was difficult to keep pace with him; and since my battalion had been detailed as advanced guard, the day would unquestionably have provided plenty of amusement. A screen of cavalry from the 19th Hussars was to have advanced in front of us, and this in itself would have been a novel experience, being the first time, I imagine, since 1914, that such a thing has been possible on the Western Front.

However a stop was put to proceedings by the signing of the Armistice, which took place in the morning, and my orders were countermanded, and the battalion sent to La Tombe. As we marched away the band played a tune well known to the men, who sang:

'When this bloody war is over,
Oh! How happy I shall be!'

This, no doubt, was very appropriate, but nevertheless, what a thousand pities that we should have had to draw off at such a moment – just as we had the enemy cold.

Private Bill Smedley
14th Battalion, Worcestershire Regiment

When ten to eleven came I was really windy! The Germans started shelling – one or two long-range stuff, expending their shells instead of carrying them back. I just threw myself under an embankment. All of a sudden I felt a crack on my steel helmet – shrapnel! It jerked my head a bit – but it didn't penetrate the helmet itself. I looked up and there was a girl at the side of me. I thought, 'My God, I've gone mad now! A damned girl beside me in the midst of a war!' Anyhow, it seems this girl was in a nearby farmhouse, heard the shelling, saw me dart under this embankment and she'd come out and done likewise! The shelling finished right on the dot at eleven o'clock! Not another thing!

Second Lieutenant Cyril Dennys
Royal Garrison Artillery

We were overlooking the Scheldt River, in a terribly exposed position, and it seemed to us that if there was a battle, we were going to have a pretty rough time of it. But before it could come, we had this news that at 11 a.m. hostilities were going to cease. We just bloody well couldn't believe it! It didn't seem that this could really be happening. Just before 11 a.m. it occurred to us that it would be very annoying to be left with loaded guns that we couldn't fire. Because unloading is an awful nuisance with big guns and you have to be jolly careful what you do. So we cocked our guns up to an angle that we felt made it certain that no-one was going to get killed when we fired, because we didn't want to slay anyone in that final moment.

Private William Gillman
2/2nd Battalion, City of London Regiment (Royal Fusiliers)

We had just had our time on rest, and were being sent forward again to relieve those who were in front of us. We had reached open ground when all of a sudden a band of horses galloped up with 'brass hats' and we were called to a halt. We were then addressed by the chief who didn't dismount – none of them did – he just waved his hands for us to stand easy, and unrolled this long white document. He had a good voice and read out, 'The Armistice was signed at eleven o'clock this morning' and gave the name of the place. We had heard rumours that morning that we'd really got Gerry on the run, so this didn't come as a surprise. In fact, there wasn't a cheer of any kind raised when he read it out. Then he just said, 'good luck', and rode off with his officers.

Lieutenant Alex Wilkinson
2nd Coldstream Guards
(from his diary)

The jolly old war has come to an end at last – and a good end too. For peace I don't care one bit, but I am exceedingly glad that we have won the war. That is the point. And thank heavens I had a really good battle before the end. I would not have missed it for anything in the whole world. It was really nice to be there in the line when hostilities ceased. It is where I really wanted to be, and one was able to appreciate it there as nowhere else.

Nurse Rosaleen Cooper
Voluntary Aid Detachment, sister of Robert Graves

We heard about the Armistice in our camp just outside Boulogne. I was on night duty, so I was allowed to take the morning off, provided I got some sleep in later, so I went into Boulogne. Oh, there was such excitement! There was a notice up on the door of the town hall which said, '*Onze heure du matin, la guerre est finie*'. Perfect strangers were hugging each other on the street and crying. Middle-aged men were hugging each other saying, '*Vous-êtes content, mon ami?*' '*Ah oui – je suis content!*' It was all very exciting.

There was immense relief all round, but especially among the British patients I'd been looking after, because all the ones who weren't very sick dreaded going back into line. I went into the mess room – and we were allowed to wear beautiful dresses there – and I sat down at the piano and I played the Chopin prelude called the 'Eleven o'clock', because it has got those great clanging eleven chords. It seemed to me a great way of celebrating the end of the war.

Fusilier Alexander Jamieson
11th Battalion, Royal Scots Fusiliers

As we advanced, we saw the terrible state of the Ypres salient. There were wrecked tanks from 1917 all over the place. I was used to dead horses and mules, but not in the numbers that we saw up there. It was just shell holes everywhere. By the end of the first day we were clear of Ypres and on a ridge where we could look ahead and see trees and a landscape that had not been affected by the war. It was just unbelievable. We knew then that things were going well.

We came back out of the line at a place called Vichte and had gone to bed in a hay loft. Our sergeant came in shouting that the war was over. Everybody got up and went down into this wee village. The *estaminet* owner opened his pub and issued free drinks and then went back to his bed.

Captain Thomas Westmacott
Royal Artillery

There was no great demonstration by the troops, I think because it was hard to realise that the war was really over. Shortly before 11 am, our Divisional Artillery let the Hun have it with every available gun. I never heard such a roar. A great contrast to the deathly silence which followed at 11 am.

Lieutenant Edward Allfree
Royal Garrison Artillery

No more shelling, no more gas, no more forward observation stunts with the infantry, no more casualties! In fact, the rest of life a holiday – that's what it seemed like then! With the war over, what else mattered? Why worry again about anything? Life without war should be blissful happiness – one long leave with no return to war at the end of it! So it seemed to me that day. The holiday spirit was upon us!

Gunner George Worsley
Royal Field Artillery

At eleven o'clock on the day itself, a trumpeter came round and sounded the 'Cease Fire', quite dramatically. I remember doing a cartwheel and I said to myself, 'I'm alive! It's all over and I'm alive!'

We went into the house of a French woman. We found her in the kitchen, furiously pulling up the flagstones in the stone floor to find a bicycle she'd taken to pieces and hidden from the Germans all through the war. She was a woman of great spirit. In fact, she didn't think the war should be over. She kept shouting, 'Berlin! Berlin!' and pointing, as much as to say we'd given up too soon. Germans had been sleeping there the night before, and she shouted, '*Pas fini! Revanche! Revanche!*' She wanted revenge. I said, '*Mais peut être je suis mort* – you know, I might get killed. She says, 'Sanfairyann', meaning that didn't matter. I said, 'Sanfairyann be buggered! I'm alive. The war's over. That's good enough for me!'

Annah Peck
American Red Cross

When the news reached us, the first impression was that a curious pall seemed to fall over everything and no-one knew whether to believe it or not, for although the announcement was quite official, the fact seemed too big to grasp. It was as if one had been holding fast to something all these years, holding on with a grip that one never dared to slacken, and suddenly one was told to let go – and as the tired muscles relaxed, they seemed to hurt more than when one was holding on. It hurt in many ways, as big events must do, but the joy of peace was there too, and as the men realized it, one saw the change.

That night in the canteen, they sang as they had never sung before – not the banal songs to pass the time, but the *Marseillaise* and *Madelon*, and the songs that they really loved. One man from the Opera with a magnificent voice sang the verses, and when the chorus came, all the *poilus* joined in and seemed to sing with open throats and hearts. It was wonderful, and that evening we did not close the canteen and put the lights out at nine o'clock, which was the rule at the Front, but let them sing until they were too hoarse to go on any longer. We stayed and listened, thrilled – for at last some expression had been given to the pent-up feelings of the day.

Dolly Shepherd
British civilian balloonist and parachutist, driver with WAAC

When the Armistice *was* announced on the 11th, it was strange. We wept because the silence was so awful – we had been used to the guns all day long, all day every day. We were so pleased to have silence at last, but we certainly made whoopee that night!

Shortly after the Armistice, I was told go and pick up the King of Belgium and take him to Bruges. When I got there he was sitting by a private plane eating bacon, cheese and pickled onions. When we got to Bruges, oh the excitement! People were giving me banknotes and things and shaking me by the hand as if I was a heroine – oh yes, that was an exciting time.

Corporal John Collins
No. 1 Cavalry Field Ambulance, RAMC

A silence came over the whole place that you could almost feel. After four and a half years of war, not a shot was being fired, not a sound was heard because the fog blanketed everything, and hung really thickly over us. We were northeast of Mons, whereas I'd started the battle four and a half years before southeast of Mons.

The feeling that we should never come under fire again was one of tremendous relief – like taking off two heavy overcoats in a humid atmosphere. The terms of the Armistice were that there had to be six miles between the German troops and our advance, and every day they were moving back into Germany and we moved after them – but there was always six miles between the two armies. That night, because we were closer than six miles to them, we moved back into Mons itself and were billeted. That evening the good people of Mons came round to our Field Ambulance and took us in sixes and fours into their homes and gave us the meal of a lifetime. They told us that they had dug up from their gardens all the food and wine they had buried four and a half years before when the Germans entered the city.

The following day, we rested, but we went back that next evening for another meal, but those two days were the only rest we had, because on the third day we started moving forward into Germany.

On the evening of the second day, the army had got the entertainers up – the comedians and the music-hall artists – and they'd taken over a theatre in Mons. It was first class entertainment and we all enjoyed it immensely – there were singers, jugglers, one-act plays – a lovely evening. There was one famous juggler – he was about six foot five, with tremendous long arms – a comic figure himself.

Nurse Alison Strathy
American Red Cross

A mob came down the Avenue de l'Opera – it developed into a procession. At its head marched Latin Quarter students, all wearing large black ties, carrying the flags of the Allied countries. They were followed by soldiers, sailors, *midinettes* – young part-time milliners or dressmakers – members of the Red Cross, the YMCA, civilians and more soldiers. In front of the Opera, the procession seemed to hesitate for a moment, then with one accord they broke into the *Marseillaise*. It was like a match to a bonfire, now we were a seething crowd celebrating victory!

I joined the parade through the streets of Paris and found myself arm in arm with *poilus* I had never seen before. I forget where we went, but we toured the streets and sang and sang, and the procession kept growing longer and longer. Finally, we ended up at the Place de la Concorde and stopped before the statue to the 'City of Lille', which was draped with flags and loaded with laurel leaves – it had been just liberated from German hands by the British. The statue to the 'City of Strasbourg' was similarly decorated, as it had been recaptured by the Americans.

Before we separated we sang *La Marseillaise* again, and more than one Frenchman had tears in his eyes.

That evening, a blind *sous-officier* was with us. After numerous toasts and speeches by all and sundry, our young soldier stood up, steadied himself by the table, and without a word, launched forth into a patriotic song. It was in gratitude for the deliverance of Lille, and for Lille he had given his sight. We kissed him goodbye and he returned to his hospital and his thoughts, and we to the crowds.

Lloyd Fox
British conscientious objector, served with Friends' Ambulance Unit

About a week before the Armistice I had a shocking cold – and I had a sore throat from inhaling gas. I was sitting in the dark with just a hurricane lantern in one of the rooms of the convent, and I thought it would do me good to put my feet in hot water, so I boiled some up on my primus stove and I was sitting with my feet in a basin of hot water when news of the Armistice reached the town.

There was lots of horn-blowing, and I forgot my cold, and my hot water and went down to the main square. I joined in as a group of people pulled the German bandstand to pieces to make a large bonfire, then we danced round it. That was the night before the official Armistice was declared at 11 the next morning, but the war was over as far as Courtrai was concerned. I had to deal with the last of my army cases – an unfortunate young soldier who was hit in the face by a star shell fired by some drunken Americans who were going round the streets, firing off their Very pistols. One of these things came down and hit this man, killing him on the spot. That was our last war casualty and the last stretcher I had to clear up.

Major Richard Russell
Royal Field Artillery

We arrived in Paris around eleven o'clock on the morning of 11th November. I stepped on to the platform and I heard a bang – somebody had fired off something to announce the return of peace. We found ourselves two rooms, had a wash and shave, then went out on to the streets. By that time, Paris had started to go a bit mad. All the shops had shut and the assistants and other workers were out on the streets, shouting and cheering. We hadn't gone very far when about a dozen girls surrounded us in a ring and we had to kiss every one of them before they'd let us go. We thought they'd gone completely mad. As we walked on, an old man with a beard ran towards me shouting, 'Anglais! Anglais!', and put his arms around me and kissed me heartily on both cheeks. This went on all over Paris, where British troops made up a very small minority of the crowd – it was all Americans.

At one point in that mad day there was a procession of students coming down a main road, headed by a British brigadier. One of the students had a long pole with a board on top, showing a cartoon of the Kaiser, running for his life with his hand over his private parts, with Madame France, a cap of liberty on her head, and carrying a big carving knife in hot pursuit.

We got some lunch at the Ambassadors on the Champs Elysées, then decided we ought to find some female company. We met two very nice girls and I asked them if they would like to have supper with us that evening. They got proper permission – there was not to be any sort of funny business attached to it – and we went off to supper at Maxime's. We got our table and then we said we must go and wash our hands. I went to one of the cubicles and as I was opening the door, an old woman pushed past me and polished up the seat with a great duster and exclaimed triumphantly, 'Go ahead, Monsieur'.

We had a very pleasant dinner, after which Jackson proceeded to stand on the table and sing 'God save the King!' At the end of the evening we took our lady friends home.

Lance Corporal Abraham
Royal Engineers

Following the gas attack, after a few days of swabbing, my blistered eyelids became less painful. Each day I was able to open them a little more, so that gradually my sight returned. It was, however, several years before I could stand strong sunlight or wind without intense discomfort.

On 9 November I was given a complete new uniform and marched – or hobbled – to a nearby convalescent camp. I found walking very painful. After so many months in the line and hundreds of miles of marching, my feet had developed a thick protective layer of hard skin. Lying in a hospital bed had caused them to crack.

Convalescent camp was designed to discourage anyone from staying there a moment longer than could be helped. We were housed in unheated Nissen huts – but I think we each had a blanket. I can't recall any sort of bed, and I think we must have slept on the floor. I was now among complete strangers from all branches of the army, changing daily as drafts left for base depots and others arrived from hospitals.

I have never ceased to be thankful for the ease with which one made friends under such conditions. Equally, of course, one took a dislike to others, but people of similar interests and outlook seemed to gravitate towards one another, sharing parcels from home and helping one another in countless ways.

I made a friend on my first day in that camp, and on 11 November – that never-to-be-forgotten day he and I were detailed for camp guard duty. Up to the previous day I think few of us had realized just how near we were to the end of the war. There was no radio in those days and we had long learnt to distrust the stuff that found its way into the few newspapers that were available to us – but on the 10th November the camp was buzzing with rumours that hostilities would cease the following day. At some time during the day a poster appeared on the camp noticeboard confirming this.

I forget when our guard duties commenced on the 11th, but at eleven o'clock that morning no–one cared. We all went crazy, including the camp cooks, so that there was no dinner for us, but what did that matter? We of the camp guard were supposed to see that no–one left the camp without a pass. Of course everyone did, and we made no attempt to stop them. The sergeant of the guard said to me, 'I'm going to bugger off until 10 p.m., and I shall expect to find you all here then.' When he had gone I told the rest of the guard we would do likewise, and although they were all strangers to me – and to one another – not one of them let me or the sergeant down. We were all there and tolerably sober when the orderly officer came round that night.

The camp was quite deserted when my new friend and I set forth and made our way down into Le Treport to do our bit of celebrating. Food and drink still had little attraction for me, but we had to do something special on such a wonderful night as this. We had a few drinks and then went into a restaurant and asked what we could have. You didn't order things in those days – you just took what was available or went without. To our surprise, the waiter said we could have steak and chips and spinach, so we settled for this with a bottle of *vin rouge*. The steak was unlike any that I had ever tasted and, at the time, I attributed this to the residual effects of mustard gas – but I have since wondered whether that was the one and only time I tasted horse, or perhaps mule.

There was a wonderful atmosphere that night – the tremendous relief at knowing we should not have to go back into the trenches or to open warfare again, was beyond my ability to describe. We finished our wine and strolled around, just enjoying the general air of happiness. We may have had a few more drinks, but although we had every excuse to have a skinful, we were certainly not tight as we made our way back to camp and our onerous guard duties.

Everyone seemed so very happy that night, and as we made our way up the hill from the centre of town, we overtook two French soldiers, each with a girl on his left arm while using his right hand to piss in the gutter. They all appeared to be drunk and were making a tremendous noise. They greeted us like brothers, but George and I broke away from the party and got back to the guardroom just in time for the inspection by the sergeant and the orderly officer.

Ruby Ord
British civilian clerk with WAACs

I think we were all expecting the Armistice – we thought it was near – but I think it was an anti-climax. Suddenly you thought of all the people you had known who had been killed. They were just in the war zone and they could come home in your imagination, but the Armistice brought the realization that they weren't coming back – that it was the end. So I think it was not such a time of rejoicing as it might have been. We were glad the fighting was over and that no more men would be killed, but it was dampened down very much in France. In England there was all this exuberance, but I think we were too near reality to feel that way.

Webb Miller
Correspondent for United Press

As the hour of eleven approached, the men kept their eyes on their wristwatches. From the direction of Verdun the fog-muffled rumble of the cannonade gradually died away. In our sector somewhere to the left there had been occasional rat-tat-tat-tats from machine guns. Now they ceased.

Eleven o'clock! The war ended!

It would make a better story if I could tell of men cheering, yelling, laughing and weeping with joy, throwing their tin hats in the air, embracing one another, dancing with delight. But they didn't. Nothing happened. The war just ended.

The men stood talking in groups. The captain let me talk on the telephone to the outposts. No drama there either. They said they couldn't see anything in the fog or hear anything. Further up the line it was the same. The army's reason for existence had suddenly ceased. The men didn't know what to do next.

Here I was, covering the greatest story in the world and nothing was happening. This was the end of the greatest war in the history of the world – the war that killed eight and a half million men, the war that affected in some way every man, woman and child on earth. And here in the front line there was less excitement, less emotion and less delirious joy than you'd find in a lively crap game.

Corporal Reginald Haine
1st Battalion, Honourable Artillery Company

It wasn't like London, where they all got drunk. No, it wasn't like that. It was all very quiet. You were so dazed you just didn't realise that from now on, you could stand up straight and not be shot.

Private James Hewitt
7th Battalion, Leicestershire Regiment

When it came, the Armistice was more than a surprise – we heard about it in shock and disbelief. We met an artilleryman out of the line and we asked, 'What's this about an armistice?' He said, 'It's all over bar the shouting!' We still wouldn't believe it, because these explosions were still going off. We wouldn't believe it until we marched into a farmyard and our officer said, 'Now you and I can breathe again – the war is over.' Beyond that there were no emotions whatsoever. We simply went into the village and lay down. I don't think we quite got it.

Corporal Clifford Lane
1st Battalion, Hertfordshire Regiment

As far as the Armistice itself was concerned, it was a kind of anticlimax. We were too far gone, too exhausted really, to enjoy it. All we wanted to do was go back to our billets. There was no cheering – no singing. That day we had no alcohol at all. We simply celebrated the Armistice in silence and thankfulness that it was all over. We were drained of all emotion. That's what it amounted to.

Captain Oliver Woodward
1st Australian Tunnelling Company

One would have expected that at this stage the field would have been filled with men carried away in a paroxysm of joy, but it was not so. Instead, officers and men moved quietly about from one group to another, giving and receiving a handshake amongst comrades. It was an occasion too great for words. The artificial barriers of rank were temporarily cast aside, and we felt to the full the real comradeship of war and the realization that the distasteful task had ended. In our mind we called to memory those of our comrades who had made the supreme sacrifice.

Corporal Arthur Atkins
14th Battalion, Machine Gun Corps

A runner from headquarters arrived, saluted our officer and handed him a message. He read it, looked at his watch, then called me over to him. He said in a most matter-of-fact, unemotional tone, 'Corporal, hostilities cease in seven minutes' time!' I saluted him and said, 'Very good, Sir!' in the same tone of voice.

When I passed the news on to my team, it was received in the same nonchalant manner, and they just carried on with what they were doing, except for saying, 'OK, Corp!' It seems absolutely extraordinary that none of us, at that stage, felt the slightest sense of relief or jubilation at the news – news that we had all looked forward to for four and a half years, and hoped to hear one day, but often thought that we would never live to hear. And now it had actually arrived, it just did not sink in at once.

Major F. J. Rice
Royal Field Artillery

When we heard about the Armistice, my officers and I bought a bottle of port. We then went round the gun park and harness sheds and told the NCOs and men. As an example of the calmness with which it was received, when we met Sergeant Goodall walking across the gun park and told him, he merely halted, saluted, said, 'Very good, sir', and walked on.

Sergeant Major Richard Tobin
Hood Battalion, Royal Naval Division

The Armistice came – the day we had dreamed of. The guns stopped, the fighting stopped. Four years of noise and bangs ended in silence. The killings had stopped.

We were stunned. I had been out since 1914. I should have been happy – I was sad. I thought of the slaughter, the hardships ... the waste and the friends I had lost.

Sapper Arthur Halestrap
Royal Engineers

I took the signal for the Armistice, yes. And, from that moment the silence was – I can only describe it as terrible. It seemed that everything dropped away from me. I thought, 'Now what will I do? There's no objective, there's nothing in front of us. I've just got to wait.' There was an absolute silence. It was indescribable.

When you have everything you'd been working for years, suddenly disappear, it seems there's no future. What is my future? What am I going to do next? Just wait for orders. I felt a sort of helplessness. We were going to have to wait to see what we're going to do next.

Sergeant Harry Hopthrow
Royal Engineers

When the Armistice came, I felt an enormous blank in my life, and wondered what I would do next, because most of my skills were involved with wireless telegraphy in the army. There was a silence in my mind as to what the future was going to be.

Private Thomas Hooker
Machine Gun Corps

We'd been a fortnight at Étaples at least, and we were there when we heard of the Armistice. At that time I didn't feel any frustration at not seeing any action, but afterwards when we found that was definitely that, and we had lost the chance of being under fire, my personal feeling was that I had missed out on something.

Mind you, it was a good miss – everybody thought it was a good miss. Someone said, 'A man thinks meanly of himself if he has never been a soldier.' Well, I was a soldier all right, but I hadn't been under fire, so I thought that meanly of myself. Oh the horrors of war – we were just youngsters – just nineteen, all of us.

Corporal Tommy Keele
11th Battalion Middlesex Regt, attached to 'Ace of Spades' Concert Party

We knew the Gerries had had it and that an Armistice would be signed on November the 11th, and we were in some little village when, at eleven o'clock, it was. We all congregated in the streets to hear the sirens go, declaring that the war was finished. Some clever ones thought they would go a bit further and they sent up rockets – the type that we would send up as a distress signal. Bert Stanley and I were standing in the street and suddenly we heard something coming – zzzooooomm ... crash – and it was one of these flaming rockets. The outer shell came down and just missed us. Had it hit our heads it would have brained us. So we nearly lost our lives on the first day of the Armistice.

Margaret Mercer
English volunteer

One cannot rejoice at such a victory – the price has been far too terrible – but at least it has not been paid in vain. And surely, even Germany will learn by this awful lesson, that war is mad and terrible, and that there are things in the world stronger and more powerful than Krupp's cannon.

I am lucky to be so much in the thick of the French Army for this wonderful day, but am surprised at the calm everywhere. There are flags on the battered houses and on most of the *camions*, but there is no singing or shouting. I think we are still too near the horrors of war there for any show of high spirits, with the hospital full as ever of crippled and dying men. There is more a feeling of immense relief than anything, and '*enfin, on ne se tue pas*' (at last the killing has stopped) is the commonest expression, which truly expresses the heart of the situation.

We are busier than usual and have hardly time to think or realise at all that this is the day we have been praying for, for four and a half years. We have an invasion of dreadful old women this evening who have been driven from a hospice that was shelled and set on fire by the retreating Boches. They've been in German hands for four and a half years and are all half-mad, either from old age or shock. It is a most trying party to cope with – far worse than hundreds of *poilus*.

Captain Charles Gee
9th Battalion, Durham Light Infantry

When we realized the Armistice was real, we had a glass of wine that night. We all felt very relieved. I wrote to my brother – but I was convinced he was dead. I reckoned I knew that he was dead on the 8th. I had been doing a lot of work in the orderly room at the time and I went to my hut and suddenly thought of my brother – a premonition that he could be dead. I wrote a card to him when the Armistice came, saying, 'I am alive are you?' – then I heard some weeks later that he was dead.

Private Jonas Hart
Essex Regiment

We were simply told that Germany had collapsed and the war was over. In the morning, we were marched down to the village and allowed to buy whatever we wanted. We could mingle with the people. The French couldn't do enough for us – they were wonderful. But we all wanted to go to our own home.

We were warned that any man found raping a woman would be immediately arrested and sent back to camp. One man was caught, and he was taken back to the camp under escort, and next morning at daybreak he was taken out and shot.

Sergeant Harry Hopthrow
Royal Engineers

After the Armistice there was some backlash against those French who had collaborated with the occupying Germans. I saw a man being marched off, suspected of being a spy. Also, on the morning of the Armistice Day in Rennes, the locals had turned out in great force and put out banners, 'Welcome to our liberators'. There was a lot of screaming going on, and we discovered they had been picking out all the girls who collaborated and were cutting off their hair. In fairness, there were two people in our lives – us and the enemy – and you were either with us or against us. I don't think nationality came into it very much.

Sergeant John Stephenson
Duke of Wellington's Regiment

The officer called me in and told me the sad news that my mother had died, and I must get ready to go home on leave. What a homecoming. I thought that I had got home before the funeral and I looked into each room to see mother – but she had been buried two days before I returned. This was something I had not thought of. There was one consolation, and that was mother was alive on Armistice Day. She knew that I was still alive, the fighting had ended and that was a crumb of comfort. I felt that a very large part of my life had vanished.

Corporal Flowers
Motor Transport Section, Army Service Corps

When we heard the Armistice was signed, we thought we'd have a bit of fun. There were a lot of small dumps about – ammunition and Very lights, so we set them alight – firing shots into them – and then of course you only wanted one to go up and all the rest went. We had a real Guy Fawkes! The officers never interfered, but a bit later, I was with the lads round the lorries and we were all jostling together, talking – having a bit of sport because all work had finished – and the officer came across to me. He says, 'Flowers, I want to have a word with you.' I thought it was about this stuff we'd blown up. He said, 'Come across to my office,' and then he linked his arm into mine – and that struck such a note in my head, because I was only a corporal and there was this officer linking arms with me!

As we got to the door of the office, he says, 'Have you had any letter from your wife of late?' I said, 'Yes, I had one yesterday, on the 10th.' My wife worked in munitions, and in this letter she told me she was taking time off to go and nurse her mother who was ill with influenza. The officer said, 'Did she say anything about feeling poorly?' I knew that influenza was raging, and it dawned on me immediately what he was going to say. I said, 'Now, don't go and tell me what I'm thinking.' 'I'm afraid I am,' he said. 'I've got a telegram here. She passed away.' Well, I just swooned into his arms. He sat me in a chair in his office and he made me take a drink of whisky. 'Now,' he says, 'I'm going to leave you here entirely on your own for a while, and I'm going off to get your leave through.' I couldn't even thank him, because I was just – out. I thought what a day it was for this to happen. Now that we can be sure we're going to get home – because there hadn't been a day in the last four years that we dared say that – and it looked as if we were all safe and going to see our homes again – now this had come.

I was on the boat next day – and of course, the leave boat, with the war being over, it was all jollification, all the lads excited. But I ran into one chap leaning over the rail. I thought he was sick at first, and then I saw he was weeping. I put my hand on his shoulder and said, 'What's the matter, chum?' And he pulled a telegram out of his pocket and showed me. Same thing! So I pulled mine out and says, 'There's a pair of us!' We stuck together, not knowing where to go, what corner to get into to get away from it all. Broken down. I've had some journeys in my life, but never one like that. To think, I'd gone the four years without a scratch except a bit of gas, and got to the end of the war – and then to lose her.

Private Arthur Wrench
51st Highland Division
(in a letter home)

To think poor brother Bill paid the penalty of patriotism so soon! I wonder what thanks he'll get for it – and we who survive too.

The celebrations here were a riot of enthusiasm – it is pandemonium and I am sure we must all be mad – but while we are letting ourselves get loose, it is certain that each one of us has time to give a thought of regret for our late pals who have 'gone west' and have not been spared to go mad like us. It is yet to be seen whether the price they have paid will be in vain or will be truly honoured and appreciated.

I think it is quite hopeless to describe what today means to us all. We, who will return to tell people what war really is, surely hope that 11 a.m. this day will be of great significance to generations to come. Surely this is the last war that will ever be between civilized nations.

PRISONERS OF WAR

As the Armistice was announced – to a mixed reception – in the trenches and all the way from the Front to the Channel coast, there were still those, detained in German POW camps, who heard only rumours of an end to hostilities. Deprived of the latest news, many were not only unsure as to whether or not the war was over, but who were also by no means certain who had won. The guards at some prison camps disappeared mysteriously, leaving their charges to fend for themselves. The freed men set out on the long trek towards the British lines, uncertain of their geographical whereabouts and fearful for their lives. Many were already weakened and ill from the privations of POW camp life, and the shortage of food and safe shelter made the journey a trek too far for some.

Corporal Hawtin Mundy
5th Battalion, Oxfordshire and Buckinghamshire Light Infantry

I was a POW in East Prussia at the time and was on good terms with the mill owner who said, 'You go down to the village and look in the window of the Post Office.' I did so, and in the window there was a telegram, written in German, and as near as I can remember, it said, *Der Krieg is fertig in der Schuzengraben* – 'The war is over in the trenches.' When I read that, I went straight back to the lager where he was billeted, and all our fellows were there. When I got back I told them, 'It's finished, boys. We've had it. We're all right now. It's all over.'

Captain C M Slack
1st/4th Battalion, East Yorkshire Regiment

We finished up in the barracks in Cologne, about three hundred of us, and not much food except what came in our parcels, and then the Armistice came along.

Then a few days after that, they were still blowing the bugle for us to go out on parade – but we didn't. We said, 'No, we've won the war. We're not going to parade any more.' One day a fellow said to me, 'Look here, Slack, we've won the war. Will you walk round Cologne with me?' I said, 'Yes,' and we polished our buttons up and walked straight out, past the sentry. Although we'd won the war, the sentries were still there. As we went out, the sentry called, 'Halt!' 'It's all right, we're coming back.' We went on slowly, half expecting to get one in the back. We went into the cathedral and stayed there for about half an hour and nothing happened – no hue and cry – and we came out, crossed the Hohenzollern Bridge and went back to the camp – and that was that.

We'd seen some of the Germans coming back with their donkey carts and their goats and kit. A regular rabble, shouting and waving to the crowds who were cheering them on, banners across the road, 'Welcome home to our unconquered heroes!'

A day or two after that, four officers went down to the station with their suitcases and asked for four tickets for London and they were told, 'We're sorry, but the lines are broken.' And so they came back to the camp.

Even though we were prisoners, we were paid. They gave us money and it was debited against our account and it was accumulating all the time – and there were three hundred of us. The senior officers went to the Cologne authorities and said, 'Look here, can't we hire a boat?' So we chartered a boat down the Rhine. We stopped at Dusseldorf for the first night and some of the people put up at hotels. I put up at the equivalent of the YMCA, and about three in the morning, a policemen was shaking my shoulder. 'Get back to the ship. They're rioting in the town.' Dusseldorf was full of 'Reds' and they were going to burn all the hotels and places where these British officers were, so we got back into our ship, sailed on to Rotterdam, and there the British authorities took us over. The next day they put us on their own boat and we landed in Hull, my old hometown, a fortnight after the Armistice. We were the first people home – and we came on our own ... we just arrived!

Colina Campbell
Voluntary Aid Detachment
(from her diary)

Such a sad thing happened about a week ago. I drove one of our British sailors who had been a prisoner in the hands of the Austrians for twenty-six months, and he had just come through on his way to England. He was so looking forward to seeing his people once more, after he had been captured off a submarine. He had a temperature and I took him into hospital and saw the doctor, and asked him not to keep him a moment longer than necessary, as the man was pining to go home. I heard yesterday that the lad had died. I just could not sleep all night thinking of him – and he is only one case out of many.

Our prisoners coming through just make your heart bleed, they look at you with such pathetic eyes and say, 'You're a woman, we could not even begin to tell you the things we have suffered.' Many of them are in such a weak condition that the first food, which people give them out of the kindness of their hearts, knocks them over. Their stomachs are too weak to stand anything.

Corporal Anthony Newman
The Essex Regiment

13 November, we rose early and I was surprised to find no German guards. They left a note in the hall saying we were to make our way to Tournai or Ath, which was the boundary our troops had to keep to for seven days, giving the Germans time to evacuate. We started off early in the morning with nothing to eat, and we were feeling very hungry. The last day in Brussels, we were given a spoonful of jam, and turnips we dug up from a field constituted our food for three days. We walked all this day and arrived at Ath about 8.30 pm. I hardly know how I did the last few miles, but about four miles out of this town, we met one of our despatch riders, and the sight of khaki cheered us up. At Ath we were told to go to the town mayor, who would find us sleeping accommodation, but I felt I could walk no more and went with two of my friends into a factory and slept on bags of shavings. Although our lads cooked supper for us, we were too far gone to get up for it. Next morning saw us lined up for breakfast early. We were given a piece of ham, bread and butter and tea. What a feed! I had seen nothing like it for ages.

Private William Easton
77th Field Ambulance, RAMC

We heard about the Armistice and they sent over guards from other camps – they thought there was going to be a bit of trouble. There was a camp with what we called the new prisoners – of which I was one. The day before the Armistice they said I could go out to work next day, but not do any work after eleven o'clock – and I could stay out if I wanted to.

I didn't know what to think, but directly the Germans heard about the Armistice, which was the night before, they left all the guard houses – in each of which they'd got two machine guns – they were frightened the prisoners might take revenge on them. Some of these fellows in the camp were regular army and had come there from Mons, and they got a hold of some of these arms. They said if any Germans came near them, they'd shoot them. I wasn't there when this happened – I'd gone out to work, and I stopped out overnight, and so did several others. During the night they rushed in cars with a whole army unit and they surrounded the place. They took the guards out over the border to Holland under escort to get them away – they thought it was going to be murder.

Private Walter Hare
15th Battalion, West Yorkshire Regiment

I was in a POW camp in Saarbrucken when we heard from civilians that the war had ended. I left the camp and set out in the direction of the river and I could see a very large city in front of me. I wanted to find some civilians who might give me a bit of bread – I was so hungry. But before I could do that, a German unit on horseback spotted me. They wanted to know where I had come from and soon they made me walk back to the school that had been our prison camp. Their commander followed me on his horse and handed me over to the guards. They pushed me into a room and after a while an officer came to interview me. He told me to stand up and face him – *'Engländer Schweinhund'*. 'English pig dog! Stand up!' So I stood up and he started threatening me. I said, 'You can't do that – the war is over.' I wasn't sure that it was. He swore at me, pulled out his revolver and pointed it at me. I thought, 'This is it, the end of the road!' He carried on shouting for a bit, but I kept quiet and I let him swear and rant at me – then when he'd finished, he whipped round and just walked off. He hadn't pulled the trigger – so I was still here. That was on Sunday the 10th.

On the 11th they kept us locked in, but let us out for a bit of exercise. While we were out, some of the villagers came around and shouted out to us, so they got us inside again. Then, towards dusk, they lined us up on the road and marched us off under guard with sentries carrying loaded rifles.

The guards' attitude hadn't changed at all – so we thought they were winners and we were still prisoners. They were certainly treating us as such. They marched us a few miles and put us into an old barracks and locked us in. It was quite dark, but we felt about and found that there were wire beds so some of us decided we'd try to get a spot of rest, as we didn't know what tomorrow might bring. We thought they would shoot us all – either that or take us to a labour camp to keep us as prisoners and make us work. We didn't get any sleep, but we did get a bit of rest, and the next morning somebody tried the door. It opened, so somebody must have unlocked it during the night. I said, 'Be careful! They've told us that we will be shot if we try to escape, so they are very likely to shoot us one by one as we go out.' We opened the door a little bit further – and nothing happened – so I volunteered to go out with another couple of chaps to see what would happen. We flung the door open and dashed out, fully expecting to be shot, but nothing happened. There were no guards anywhere to be seen. The place was absolutely empty.

We set out on foot, but we didn't know where we were, we had no food, no money, and we didn't know what to do. There were four of us – me and my brother, a lad called Jack and this fellow Lickard. Then I saw a priest walking down the village street so I said I'd go and ask him where we were. This chap could talk a little bit of French and I could talk a little bit of German, so I was able to make him understand that we wanted to get away. The only place I could think of was France, so I asked him, 'How do we get to France?' 'France?' He looked at me and repeated, 'France?' I said, 'Yes.' He asked if we had any money or food – and I said we hadn't. 'So how will you get there?' I said we'd have to walk – there was no any other way.' He told me that France was over a hundred miles away, but I said, 'All the same, we'll have to walk. We can't stay here. Which way do we go?' He pointed down the road and he said, 'West'. I went back to the lads and told them the news. I said, 'We can't stay here – we have no food and the guards have left us. We have to get to France. Can anybody think of anything better to do?' They couldn't, so the four of us set off to walk it. We still hadn't worked out who had won the war. In fact, we felt sure we had lost.

The first two nights we slept in a hedge – then the third night it was raining. It had been a very wet day and Jack was feeling very poorly, but we kept walking. Soon he became so ill we decided to rest at the side of the road. We had a rest, then my brother went to have a look at Jack. He came back and said, 'Jack is no more bother – he is gone. He's dead.' I suppose it was just exposure and lack of nourishment. We couldn't do anything for him, so we just had to leave him.

We all had our POW numbers painted on our backs and we hoped somebody would find Jack and the number would identify him. We were very despondent because we couldn't do anything for him. We couldn't do anything for ourselves either. We didn't dare scrounge food because we were in enemy territory as far as we knew. We were still in Germany – and if we had lost the war – which was what we had expected – if anybody caught us they'd take us back to prison, to a labour camp or something worse. We wanted to get away to France as soon as we possibly could.

We came to a few unoccupied houses at the roadside. We checked them out to see if there was any food, but we couldn't find any. Some while later we came across a quartermaster's stores full of all sorts of stuff. I got a pair of binoculars and my brother got some useful equipment. Then we realized we couldn't carry it all – we had enough to carry ourselves without any extra weight. It was getting late at night so we decided to stop there overnight. We chose a house at the end of the row – checked it all over again to see if there was any food, but there wasn't. Then my brother called out that there was a cellar. He went in and came back with two bottles of wine. There was a little mug on the mantelpiece and I got it down and we were just going to have a drink when I remembered that the retreating Germans had left poisoned wine in some of houses. Some of our chaps had drunk it and that was the end of them. I said, 'No! Don't drink it! It could have been left on purpose – it will have been poisoned.' So we put the bottles down, but after a bit somebody said, 'Let's try it – see if it's all right.' Somebody had a sip – and we watched them to see if anything happened. Nothing did, so we finished off the wine and had a good night's rest afterwards. We woke up the next morning feeling a bit fuzzy, but we set off in good form – we had some stamina now, and we soon worked it off.

As we walked, we avoided any main roads and took a circular route to avoid being seen. We didn't want to be recaptured. We were three – and we wanted to remain that way.

On one occasion we heard a band playing as we were walking along the road. We got behind a hedge and waited, and after a time there was a company of German troops marching past with a band in front of them. They were all singing and shouting so we realized then that we had lost the war, because they were all so jolly. We agreed that it was a good job we'd got out of sight, because they might have done us in. Shortly after that we reached the first lot of trenches. We climbed across the barbed wire into no-man's-land and saw that there was nobody about. We looked around us, and it was complete devastation. It was absolutely terrible, and we realized that nobody would want to go there again for years to come.

We had no idea where we were. We knew we had got into France because there were French uniforms and bits of French equipment lying about. Ahead of us we saw a forest. I was the fittest of the three of us – although we were all in pretty bad shape – and I suggested that we walk around the edge of the wood. I thought we shouldn't go inside the wood because we'd get lost. We'd gone about half a mile when my brother fell into a shell hole. He was absolutely exhausted and said that he couldn't go any further. He said we should go on and find somebody that might be prepared to help us. I said, 'No – I am not leaving you.' Then Paul flopped down and said 'I can't go any further either, Walter. I'm done for.' I said, 'Here's what we'll do. We'll have ten minutes' rest, then we will get up and try and push on in a bit.' Then I lay down to rest with them – but I knew I'd never get up again – and nor would Paul or Seth. As I was lying there, I thought to myself, 'I wonder if they'll ever find us – perhaps in a few years to come. By that time we will be in such a condition they won't just not be able to tell that we were British troops on our way home – they won't even know we were human beings.' How long we lay there, I'll never know, but suddenly we heard the whistle of a railway engine. We all three jumped up – we got some strength from somewhere. We listened and it came again, and stupidly, we dashed into the wood.

Eventually we found a road and set off along it. I don't know how far we had gone – it was heavy going because we were all limping – but eventually we saw two figures in uniform ahead of us. We decided it would be better to give ourselves up – we couldn't last any longer, so we'd just have to give in. So we kept going forward and when we got near to them it was quite dusk, so it was hard to see who they were, but we found they were two French soldiers. We tried to explain who we were, but they wouldn't believe us. We turned around and said, 'Look! We've got our POW numbers on our backs!' We were able to speak a bit of French, and we explained what we'd been through. They were very upset and took us back to a hut. They were only the advance party on the edge of this wood and all they had to offer us was a drink of water – but we were glad of anything. They said they'd take us to their HQ a mile or two away at Luneville – but we said we didn't think we could walk it.

They took us there in a transport, and it was there that these lads told us, 'The war is over – and we have won!' 'Won?' 'Yes, we won!' They told us that we'd walked from Saarbrucken all through Alsace-Lorraine – and we said that we thought we were still in Germany. They said, 'Officially you still are – but it has got to be handed back. The Germans took it from France after the Franco-Prussian War and now it must be returned to France.' They called their sergeant and he woke up the cooks and told them to make us something to eat. They hadn't much to offer until they got their rations in the morning – but they gave us a cup of real coffee – no milk or sugar of course, but it was real coffee – and some sausages. It was the best sausage and coffee I have ever tasted in my life!

We'd survived, but we were in a terrible state – filthy from six days' long walk. We managed to clean ourselves up a bit before we left, so we didn't look quite as bad as we had been. They moved us on to Nancy, where there was an American Army Air Force station, and there they gave us baths, shaved us and cut our hair – made us into human beings again. They gave us food too, but we were warned not to overdo it after so long without eating. They got some British uniforms sent up for us, so we managed to get properly dressed as soldiers again. We stayed with them for two days, then they got a hospital train up there. I came down on a stretcher with a nurse to keep an eye on me.

All through this, I kept those binoculars from the quartermaster's store – and the little mug from the house with the cellar, that I drank wine from. When I got back to the British Army again, they tried to take it off me, but I said I was keeping it – it was my souvenir, and I was going to take it home. I had a job taking it back, but I got it home, and my son has it now. I explained to him that people might not know what this is all about – but that he would know the story. The binoculars, on the other hand, I sold to a woman in Nancy to get enough money to send a telegram home to tell them I was on my way back.

We got to Calais, the British red caps kept my brother behind, because he'd got a uniform, but he hadn't got a cap. He was right next to me and I said, 'He's my brother – we want to go home together.' But it didn't matter – he was back with the British Army now, and he had to be properly dressed. When I got home, my mother asked me, 'Where's your brother?' and I said I expected he'd be coming home later. She said, 'I know you – you've been telling me in your cards that he's alive – but he's not is he?' I said, 'He is,' but she insisted, 'I know he isn't, because I have had a man here from his regiment – and he said he buried him at 333 Cemetery.' I promised her that he hadn't, because he'd been with me. She said, 'Look, I've got the letter here, that I'd written to him. This was the letter they found on him.' I realized then what had happened, and explained, 'When we were holding the line, a friend of his was coming up to give him a letter – and he got killed on the way. It was a lad called Isleworth, a pal of his, so he will have been buried under the wrong name.' Later, when he finally got back, my brother went to the War Office and told them that he had a grave in 333 Cemetery in his name, and it wasn't his.

Sergeant Hawtin Mundy
5th Battalion, Oxfordshire and Buckinghamshire Light Infantry

On a visit to a British POW camp hospital in November 1918, one of the Germans came to me and he said, 'There are two of your English chaps dead. Would you bring one or two of your mates and bury them?' I said we would, and four of us went. The German took us down to a mortuary in the camp which had been dug underground, so that you had to go down some steps to get into it. It was covered over like an old-fashioned dugout in the ground. When we got there we saw there was just an ordinary dirt floor – and lying in the middle of it were nine or ten bodies – all of them stark naked. He pointed out two of them to me. 'These are your two Englishmen – all these others were Russians.' These bodies were spread out all over the floor – it was a terrible sight seeing them all laid out there. There was one that I noticed particularly – they had cut his throat and laid him on top. They hadn't even had the decency to wash the blood off. Instead they'd let it run all down on to his chest. Oh blimey, what a sight!

The German said, 'You will find some coffins,' and he took us to pick them up – but they weren't coffins at all – they were just long boxes. Anyway, we took them back and put one body in each box. The blooming things were so short, the feet hung out at the ends. Never mind – we put them on this truck and he led us up to where the cemetery was. We put these two chaps in the ground – but there was no burial service at all. We didn't know who they were – in fact we didn't even ask. All we knew was they were two of our own. So we filled in the ground and left them. I wonder if their families ever knew what happened to those blokes – it wasn't a very nice end.

We began to get a little bit anxious as to what was going to happen, it was getting towards the end of November, and the winter had set in and it was very, very bad.

Eventually we were called together one day, but it wasn't all of us – which was strange because there was a whole mob of us. The names were all called out and fortunately I was one of them. They organized for us to leave from the station at Hielsburg. It was quite a long journey to get to Danzig, although the lads thought nothing about it. On the way we pulled up somewhere, and I walked up to the engine-driver, who gave us some boiling water for our tea.

When we got to Danzig, the train went right up to the docks – and there was this Red Cross ship, with all those wonderful lads, lined up along the side of it. We got out and stood waiting in rows with all our packages and belongings – and unbelievably, there were civilians there, women and children, and they come along and they begged from us. So I tipped my pack upside down – there were a few tins of this and that, bits of bread – and they grabbed it. It was very much the same as how we had struggled in prison camp, but now it was the reverse. Almost all of us emptied our packages out because we knew we wouldn't want the stuff any longer. There was just one – a big lad, and I'll never forgive him – never. He took his box of food and walked away from the lines, snapped it open and dropped it into the sea, and said, 'Let the buggers get in and fight for that.'

We got on board and we found a number of former prisoners who had suffered from lice during the war – and some in the eastern sector, where we'd been, hadn't received any Red Cross parcels and were very thin and weak. Some of the worst of them had been taken into the hospital sick bay. The remainder of us sat down to lovely food. There was hot food, tablecloths, knives and forks! It was marvellous. I was taken down to where the cabins were – and there were lovely beds. I lay there quite a while before I went to sleep. I had a good night's sleep and when I woke up in the morning, I got dressed, then sat on my bunk putting my shoes on. Then gradually I went forward a little, and then back a little – and I thought, 'Blimey here we go! Seasickness!' I made a beeline for the deck for some fresh air, and there were quite a lot of men up there with the same problem.

When evening came, they had some musicians on board to entertain us. They'd got plenty of instruments and I played a bit with them. I love a good band, and we all enjoyed the singsong. Then, when the sea was calm, I used to love getting at the back of the boat and watching the wake. Eventually we got into Copenhagen, and it was night when we got into the harbour. It was all lit up, and it looked so beautiful. It was spectacular. We were stopping so they could load up with food again.

One of the very weak lads died. It was a very sad thing. He had to be buried at sea. The band came on deck, and one of the former prisoners who was a parson in peacetime said he would conduct the service. They brought his coffin up, laid it down, recited the service, then they gently slid the coffin over and it went 'plop' into the sea. Then the band started to play. Even years later it upsets me to talk about it.

We arrived outside Leith five days later. It was night time, so we lay outside the harbour until the morning when we could go in. It was a clear day, and I could see the railway, and what looked like toy trains. Slowly we pulled into the dock, close to the side, and there were women shouting. All the way along the dock they had a Scottish regimental band, and the whole lot of us on that boat just went mad! We couldn't help it – we clapped and hollered – it was such a very impressive sight, and you didn't know what you were doing because you were so excited.

We went into this long warehouse where there were waiting civilians. It was mainly women, and some found husbands, some found sons – but then there was the tragedy. It just made you weep – there were women there, looking for husbands, women looking for their sons. It didn't matter who it was, if someone approached me I just hugged them – but they had photos with them. Had we seen them? They would know that their man was alive because their mates sent letters – but then they weren't on the boat.

Our destination was Ripon in Yorkshire, which was a POW dispersal camp. We travelled through the night – and it wasn't spacious. On the platform was a Scotsman, who said, 'Who are you lot?' We said we were prisoners of war, coming down from Scotland, so he opened a bottle of whiskey and said, 'Have some of this.' That slipped down beautifully!

Eventually we got to the camp at Ripon and we started to mix in. They asked around, 'Have you got any specific complaints that the Germans have been cruel to you?' What a bloody silly thing to ask! They gave us a kit bag, a lovely blue-grey coat – I used that long after the war – lovely coat it was. We were told that if we wanted to apply for a pension we had to write two or three days before attending an examination – but if we didn't want a pension we could have £2 and go home the next day with our passes paid for. But if we wanted a medical examination, we weren't entitled to the couple of quid.

Well, just think what you could do with two quid in those days! The next morning we woke up with a fat head – and this is what's made me mad ever since. If someone had caught the flu or had a bit of a heart attack, they had a pension for life. I had been wounded three times, been a prisoner of war – and never had a bloody penny: I should have had that examination.

We had a repatriation period of three months in all, and there was the allowance to live on when we were demobbed, and everybody got £20. We exchanged addresses to write to each other when we got home. We were all going to have a reunion on May 3rd – but it never materialized. Once we got home we forgot everyone. I did have an address of my old French mate who lived in Lille, but I never did write to him.

Corporal Anthony Newman

Prisoner of War

We embarked on the liner *France* for Dover – great excitement on reaching home! Being Sunday, there were many people waiting for us and we were the first batch of prisoners to reach England. The Prince of Wales met us and entertained us to a feed in the Station Hall. He gave a fine speech on behalf of the King (who regretted he could not attend). The King sent us (846 of us in all) a parcel containing pipe tobacco, cigarettes, chocolate and toffee. From here we were conveyed in private motors to the North Wall camp. The streets along the way were lined with enthusiastic crowds and they greeted us wildly. Each man was given a hospital bed with wool mattress. Oh, the joy! We spent three days there, getting the necessary papers and passing the doctor, then we went by special train to Birmingham. We arrived about 4 p.m. – no reception! No-one knew who we were. A man asked me if I had come back on leave! But the next day the Lord Mayor had the police band at New Street Station to welcome the next batch – supposed to be the first prisoners home!

We were given two months' sick leave, then had to return to Shoreham-by-Sea for demobilization. Thus ended my three and a half years as a soldier of the King.

Ada Croft

Civilian

My brother Arthur and my sister Addy's husband were prisoners of war in Germany, and we didn't hear anything about them, whether they were dead or alive. We'd come back from church on Sunday evening, then continue to sing hymns at home. One Sunday, we'd all been singing hymns and there was a knock at the front door – it was Addy's husband, who nearly fell in through the door, he was so weak.

While he was away, Addy had had their baby, but while she was carrying the baby she'd been really worried about him because she'd heard he was a prisoner of war. When her baby was born she'd fretted so much that she lost it – and that's the first thing he asked when he got in – 'Where's the baby, Addy? So that really upset everyone.

CHAPTER 2

The Armistice at Home

Every family in Britain had been touched in some way by the war. Some had lost sons, fathers, brothers – and others had received back the broken shells of the men they had waved off to the war with such optimism. But the announcement of the Armistice gave the people at home a reason to rejoice – the killing was over and celebrations broke out across the country, with the greatest gathering of all in the centre of London, where servicemen and women joined with civilians, partying in the streets and celebrating into the night.

Lieutenant Richard Dixon
Royal Garrison Artillery

We were on a boat entering Folkestone harbour to go on leave when, at about midday, every craft with a siren sounded it. Everyone wanted to know what the fuss was about – then all the crews on the ships in the harbour started cheering and waving. 'Dickie,' said Captain Brown, 'the bloody war's over! It's over!' And it was. We had left France with a war on, and arrived in Blighty with a peace on! And all those ships were letting off those sirens for us, as if we were a lot of conquering heroes coming home – that was the first intimation we had of it.

While we were going through the formalities of disembarking, a strange and unreal thought was running through my mind. I had a future. It took some getting used to, this knowledge. There was a future ahead for me – something I had not imagined for some years. I said as much to Captain Brown. He smiled at me;

he was a man of about forty. 'Yes,' he agreed. 'You've got a future now, Dickie. And so have I. I wonder what we'll do with it, and what it will be like – because, you know, things are not going to be the same as they were.'

No more slaughter, no more maiming, no more mud and blood, and no more killing and disembowelling of horses and mules – which was what I found most difficult to bear. No more of those hopeless dawns with the rain chilling the spirits, no more crouching in inadequate dugouts scooped out of trench walls, no more dodging of snipers' bullets, no more of that terrible shell fire. No more shovelling up bits of men's bodies and dumping them into sandbags; no more cries of 'Stretcher-bear-ERS!', and no more of those beastly gas masks and the odious smell of pear drops which was deadly to the lungs – and no more writing of those dreadfully difficult letters to the next-of-kin of the dead.

There was silence along the miles and miles of the thundering battlefronts from the North Sea to the borders of Switzerland. There would be silence in Ypres, and over the whole haunted area of the dreaded Salient. This silence must seem positively uncanny. At long last that tormented city with the appalling ruins of its once-lovely Cloth Hall was freed from the menace of the Hun. At long last its innumerable defenders were justified and those who died in its defence could be appeased. The City of Fear was no longer the City of Fear, and doubtless out of her ruins would rise another city – a city of the new times we had hoped we were fighting for. The ancient ramparts at the infamous Menin Gate would no longer harbour our troops. The whole vast business of the war was finished. It was over.

Gunner Sidney Edwards
Royal Garrison Artillery

Because of burns I had received to my legs, I was among the wounded on board a Union Castle Line ship, crossing from Le Havre to Southampton on the night of the 10th to 11th November. Late on the morning of the 11th, as I stood in the queue to leave the vessel, news was brought aboard that Armistice had been declared. *What* a day to reach 'Blighty'!

On landing, we were taken to the train. Our destination was, to us, unknown. Scenes along the line were indescribable. Excitement was rife. Church bells were ringing and flags flying. The news had brought people from their homes, and they were gathered together, talking excitedly, while children ran wildly about.

On arrival at Eastleigh, the wounded detrained and were walked – I cannot say marched – through the streets to a nearby suburb where the temporary hospital was situated. Sympathetic remarks were made as we straggled along in our 'blues', carrying little bundles containing all that was left of our possessions. It was a great day for everyone. For myself, although my wounds were still painful, they were but slight compared with those that had brought me back to Blighty in 1917, and I was once again in the old country.

Corporal Bertram Neyland
Royal Engineers

Our first posting was in Ireland, and we felt we were in a different war altogether. We were sorry for all the boys in France and damned glad we weren't there with them. I was transferred to Buttevant in County Cork – a little village in the north of the county with a big British barracks, and the Westmoreland and

Cumberland Yeomanry were there. They were mobilized in August 1914 and they had never been out of Britain. It was weird and wonderful – they were fine physical types, but they'd never been abroad or seen action.

While I was at Buttevant, a number of things happened, but the most remarkable was the Armistice: it was the culmination of all our hopes for four years. We were receiving the news on a little home-made set that no wireless operator would have given tuppence for. The day before we had a good idea that something was going to happen. We had a miserable old pessimist with us, Jock, and he wouldn't believe that the Armistice was going to happen. He said, 'If you get definite news during the night, you can throw me out of bed.' Well, I was on watch that night and I got the news around three or four o'clock in the morning, so I shook up the other operator – there were three of us – and said, 'Jock has told me to chuck him out of bed.' So three or four others carried Jock's bed with Jock in it, out of the front door, out on to the parade ground. It was a field, and the grass was long at our end and it was raining, and we threw him out on to the wet grass, but he didn't mind.

Later in the day, the Westmoreland and Cumberlands came crowding round the door, 'Is it true, is it true?' The rain had stopped, so we carted out our table with our tuppenny set on it and we had an enormous aerial, the length of a football field and very high. We were picking up the Eiffel Tower transmitter on it quite distinctly as it broadcast the details of the Armistice to the world, repeating it all day long on the eleventh. I got the adjustments fixed to give it the maximum volume. I had two earphones, and I put them on the table so all the chaps could hear the signals. These were all clickety-clicks for the Morse code, and these chaps wouldn't believe that they were coming from the Eiffel Tower. When we wrote down what they were saying, it was in French, which added to the confusion. I remember one chap digging at someone saying, 'The war is over. Look! Hear those noises? They are coming from Paris!'

That was marvellous, then about midday everything was signed, sealed and settled. We put the sentries on the barrack gates and crowds of us went into the village. There were little shops where the women did bacon and eggs for us – and beer. We just ate bacon and eggs and drank beer until we were stiff. That night a woman from the Church Army came over to me and said, 'Mr Neyland, I'd like you to come to the garrison church with me and pray.' I was struck by the sincerity of this woman, so off I went. The two of us went to the church and prayed and gave thanks for the end.

Nurse Edith Evans
Red Cross

On the actual Armistice Day, the telephone rang at eight o'clock in the morning, and I rushed to answer it, but another nurse got there first. She called out, 'It's over – they've rung us up from Deal Pier to tell us it was going to be over at eleven o'clock.' I hurried upstairs to tell the patients, who were very excited. One picked me up and nearly flung me downstairs with excitement. The news passed round the hospital very quickly. It was a wonderful feeling of relief. We didn't have any celebration at eleven o'clock because we were deep in our dressings and work, but it happened to be the day of our concert – so it became a rather special concert and some of the men who could, struggled down on their crutches into Deal, hitting tin pans and singing – they made quite a little band – and they came back in time for the concert – although one of them certainly retired to bed. But they behaved simply marvellously – it was quite remarkable. The man who retired to bed wept to the matron next day that he'd let the hospital down – I thought that was very touching.

Private Basil Farrer
Army Pay Corps

I remember Armistice Day – and I've still got the Nottingham paper from that day. I didn't know at the time, but in every city everybody went mad, and in London the crowds were dancing in the streets. In Nottingham's Market Square there was just one mass of people, dancing and singing. I did not go along. I do remember for some reason, hard to explain in a chap as young as myself, I felt sad.

Lieutenant John Nettleton
2nd Battalion, Rifle Brigade

The 11th November was my birthday and the Armistice was the best birthday present any man ever had. I went down to the Promenade at Cheltenham and saw all the people milling about the streets singing and dancing, but even so it was impossible to realise that the war that had been going on since the beginning of time was really over. I don't think I realized it till I got on the leave train at Victoria to go back to France and found that it was just another railway journey. Always before, at seven o'clock in the morning, Victoria Station had been a very grim place, with people wrapped in their own private griefs and nobody taking any notice of anyone else. Now it was just a railway station and the goodbyes were *au revoirs*, not *adieux*!

Private Raynor Taylor
Welch Regiment

We went up to London. We didn't have to buy a rail ticket – it was free. It was chaos – the buses, many with open tops, were full of people. All the vehicles were smothered with people celebrating.

My brother was still missing at the Front, which was sad, but for me, like everybody else, the war was over. We all had a couple of jars and that was enough to lift my spirits – and there were plenty of people getting drunk. I got the impression that people in uniform could have anything – mind you, there seemed to be more people in uniforms than there were civilians! The soldiers, sailors and the auxiliary forces had the freedom of the city! We had no money, but we could still get a meal or a sandwich. It was one mad, silly celebration.

When we got back to our guard duties at the POW camp no-one was put on a charge for being absent – everybody's discipline had gone by the board. The prisoners were as elated as we were, and it caused us some concern that they thought they'd be going home the very next day. That couldn't possibly be – there was no transport. We wanted transport ourselves, to bring our fellows home – and the demand was so great that they couldn't even provide transport for our own POWs.

Captain Osbert Sitwell
Grenadier Guards

That night it was impossible to drive through Trafalgar Square – because the crowd danced under lights turned up for the first time in four years. The last occasion I had seen the London crowd was when it had cheered for its own death outside Buckingham Palace on the evening of the 4th of August 1914; most of the men who had composed it were now dead. It was an honest, happy crowd, good-natured, possessed of a kind of wisdom or philosophy, as well as of a perseverance which few races knew.

Frederick Robinson
Civilian, from his diary

November 11! A day never to be forgotten! The day has come at last which we have lived for these long four years and three months. The horrible thing is over! The last of our enemies is beaten; her once mighty Emperor is a fugitive and his Empire crumbling to the dust. It is difficult to believe all this, but it is true.

Practically all work was suspended, and the streets became packed with people, including great numbers of soldiers on leave and thousands in hospital blue – and most of these, accompanied by their lady friends, shouted themselves hoarse and waved flags, made a lot of noise on improvised instruments. Others danced informal quadrilles – all was one vast pandemonium. Perhaps such crowds have never before been seen in London.

In the Mall was an exhibition of hundreds of cannons captured from the enemy, which formed a very appropriate background to the crowds. In front of Buckingham Palace was one vast flock of people, many of whom had found positions of advantage on Queen Victoria's monument just opposite. When the King and Queen appeared from time to time on the balcony of the Palace, the enthusiasm simply knew no bounds, and later, when the King, Queen and Princess Mary (dressed as a VAD) drove down the Mall in an open carriage, the people simply went wild with delight. No Bolshevism here!

As darkness drew on, we realized that the lighting regulations had been withdrawn, and though there had not been time to clean the black shading off most of the street lamps, this had been done in some areas, and the streets, particularly Piccadilly, were comparatively well lit. The clubs and hotels had their outside lights on and their blinds up, which added to the general brightness. Passing the Houses of Parliament on our way home, we saw the great clock once more illuminated, and heard the thundering tones of Big Ben reverberating the great fact of peace.

Mabel Brown
Civilian working in printing works

We went mad – that's the only word you can use to express it. We'd got a fire-escape door at the end of the room – and we knew they were going to put a flag up outside the Crawford pub when the Armistice was declared, so somebody was detailed to open the door occasionally and look out. The flag went up and we went mad! Some of us used spanners and some used hammers for the job, and we were biffing and banging about. The boys all came rolling out of the LMS Works and somebody shouted down from our room, 'Come and fetch us out!'

Of course you had to consider the people's feelings who'd lost someone. We'd got one or two girls in the department whose brothers were not coming back. Give the girls their due, those whose boys weren't coming back, they rejoiced to think it was over and joined in with anything that went on. We thought they were wonderful.

Marie Pankhurst
Civilian
(in a letter to Corporal A.D. Pankhurst, 56th Division, Royal Field Artillery)

Everywhere closed down and no more work was done that day. Then the town was thronged with thousands of people giving vent to their feelings, and it was a wonderful sight. I only wished you had been here to witness it – or rather to have joined in. Every vehicle was chartered, private, cars, taxis, right down to a brewer's dray, including buses, government lorries of every description – and all were packed with people making merry with rattles, bells – anything that made a noise. The great place was to sit on the top of the taxi, and to see who could wear the most flags! No class distinction, Army etiquette – officers and men were one, and everyone's most awfully happy. I saw an officer changing hats with a sailor and a well-dressed woman in beautiful furs hugging the Colonials in a procession! There was such a lot of amusement – a greengrocer's cart going down the Strand was commandeered, heaps of people scrambling on. The poor driver – an old man – looked as though he thought the world was coming to an end, and sat helplessly gazing at the 'young wimmin' and comparing them to 'his day'. Eventually he gave it up as a bad job and drove on, while his companions pelted people with his Brussels sprouts. One officer getting into a taxi had a fresh herring smack on the side of his face, while some scrambled on to the top and danced. Some sat on the step, the back, and even the mudguard.

One incident amused me very much. One girl of our Corps was driving a car down Bedford Street, and had some Colonials with her. Another car going along the Strand with more Colonials and RAF girls in, was noticed by them – and one girl in particular they fancied – so they drove their car into the RAF, sprang out, collared the girl of their choice, the others trying to keep her back – but they won, carried her back, 'pitched' her into their car and drove off with her amidst a din of applause. It really is impossible to describe it. Towards night it rained – and even that did not disperse the crowds. It was carried on for a week, with fireworks and bonfires in the Square.

Mrs Maude Cra'ster
Civilian

We were in full view of the balcony. I can't tell what the sight was! Lorries crammed with men and women, all with flags – people crammed on the top of taxis and inside too. Large Government motors with hospital nurses, WAACs, and WRENs and soldiers, and the mass of all kinds on their feet. There we all waited with bated breath. Presently there was a great to-do, for mounted policemen pushed the crowd in front of them to let the bands through to the Quadrangle.

Directly the bands got into position, they struck up 'God Save the King', and he and the Queen, Princess Mary, the Duke of Connaught and Princess Patricia appeared on the balcony. I think Queen Alexandra was there too. The roar as they appeared was one roll and everyone sang with the bands. Then the King said something – but of course we couldn't hear – and then the band played 'All People that on Earth do Dwell', and everyone sang again. Then the band struck up 'Home Sweet Home', and it was this that touched the crowd, really. It was solemnly sung, almost with a sob, and I felt it a moment never to be forgotten.

After that, the English reserve gave way and they sang 'For He's a Jolly Good Fellow!' Then 'Tipperary' was played and after that, the different anthems – and then again, everyone sang with the bands, 'Now Thank We All Our God'. After that, the National Anthem was played again and the cheers roared and roared, then the Royal Family went in.

Olive Wells
Age 13, attending Streatham Secondary School

We came to school this morning hardly realising what a great day this was going to be.

Miss Basset told us that the Armistice was signed. We cheered until we were hoarse.

At 11 a.m. the guns were fired, the church bells were rung, sirens were sounded – we did not think of air raids, as we would have done on any other day.

We went out into the road and cheered. The Union Jack was sent up the flagpole and there it fluttered in the breeze. Our home-work was excused for the week.

George Cook
Schoolboy

Just after dinner, on an ordinary school day, all of a sudden the young chaps from the works burst into the school. They knocked the headmaster over and they beckoned all of the kids out of the classrooms, and believe me, we didn't need any encouragement. We all flew out and the staff were just left standing there. Then we marched behind the band all the way round the town, and I remember that as the band was marching round Wolverton, there were people all over the place, waving tiny Union Jacks. As a child I remember wondering wherever could they have got those from in such a short time?

Viva Chappill
Schoolgirl

I was at the Moon Street School then, and I remember the Armistice Day very clearly, because there was a vendetta between the apprentices in the works and our sixth formers – they used to come up snowballing if there was any snow about – but on Armistice Day they all came out of the works. As soon as they heard the Armistice was declared, they downed tools and came out and marched up to us in a group, and went all round the school, banging on the windows. 'Let them out, the war's over! Let them out!'

The senior mistress said, 'Right girls, get your coats and hats on. Put on your gloves. Go out two by two,' which we did. And as we came out they banged us each on the head – well, they were a nasty lot. They were very much against our sixth formers. If there was any snow on the ground there were snow fights. Oh yes, there was ill feeling!

Lieutenant William Benham
Royal Air Force

I was back in England – so it wasn't so easy to see what was happening on the Front. I was training to be a pilot in the air force, because I couldn't march any more because of the injury to my foot, but I think the Armistice came rather suddenly to some people. But we did feel it had been rather engineered, because it was the eleventh hour of the eleventh day of the eleventh month – we felt that they had worked it that way.

Sybil Morrison
Ambulance driver in London

Strangely, when people's sons or husbands were killed, they were not so much resentful, as proud. It was the only thing left for them. They were so young, just boys of twenty and twenty-one. I think their parents had to feel proud of them otherwise it would have been unbearable. I don't remember anyone who was resentful about the war. I think everybody had become convinced that this was necessary – and once you've started to fight a war, and the two sides are locked in battle, it's not very easy to stop it. In fact, I don't know how we did stop it. But when it *did* stop, Armistice Day, it was insane. People crowded into the streets, gathered round Buckingham Palace, stood up on the tops of buses. Traffic was at a standstill and you couldn't move – everybody was cheering, singing, shouting, and of course immensely, enormously, relieved. But the awful thing was that there were some people who were killed on that very day, while we were rejoicing. If you still had anybody at the Front, you couldn't really celebrate yet.

I went out among the crowds – I was enormously relieved. I was only too thankful to think it was over. Not that you could do anything very much – I remember being jammed up against the steps of the National Gallery. Once you were there, you couldn't move and it would have been pretty dangerous to try to. People flocked to the Palace, stood outside and just shouted. It was extraordinary. There were no speeches, just throngs of people cheering, waving flags, standing up on the top of buses.

Nurse Annie Esler
Red Cross

On Armistice Day, the pathetic part was all the poor soldiers – they were allowed to go off when peace was declared – all the ones that could were allowed to go, but a lot couldn't move so couldn't go. They were all in tears because they knew the rest of their lives was going to be miserable.

Robert Saunders
Headmaster of Fletching School, Uckfield, Sussex
(in a letter to his son)

The war has pressed more heavily on us than is generally thought, even by ourselves, and I am afraid has aged us more than the four and a half years warrant as regards time. I think most people feel that some time must elapse before we can properly celebrate peace, our feelings have been too much harassed and our sympathies too often called forth, for the losses of our friends and neighbours. As I look back, I can see so many tragedies in families I know well, and I can see so many of my old boys who are dead or wounded, or dying of consumption, and recall them as boys at school where I used to urge them on the duty of patriotism, so that at present it doesn't seem right that those who have escaped shall give themselves up to joy days.

CHAPTER 3

After the Battle

Once the reality of peace had sunk in, the men and women at the Front hoped, with few exceptions, for a speedy return home. As they served out their time before being repatriated or demobilized, there was administrative business to attend to, both in liberated France and Belgium and in defeated Germany. An army of occupation was ordered across the border into Germany to oversee the implementation of peace. Work began on the great cemeteries – the cities of the dead of all nationalities – where the remains of the fallen, identified and unnamed, would be reburied and commemorated.

Still on duty in billets near the scenes of the fighting, other servicemen had the gruesome and hazardous duties of retrieving human remains from the battlefields, collecting up abandoned guns and ammunition, and risking their lives among what often proved, fatally, to be still live shells. With a terrible and cruel irony, a virulent strain of flu swept across the continent, killing men in their droves as they awaited repatriation. The casualty list of the Great War was still not closed.

Annah Peck
American Red Cross

One day we had not gone very far before we saw hundreds of men coming towards us on the road. They were an extraordinary sight, for instead of the mass blue or khaki that one expected to see, here was a straggling line of men wearing every kind of uniform that the Allies had used since 1914. One would see many khaki figures of English Tommies and American Doughboys tramping along side by side with French *poilus* in blue and Italians in their greeny-grey uniforms, and then to our surprise, Frenchmen would appear with the old red cap and trousers, and sprinkled among all of these were men in the drab-looking uniforms worn by the Allied prisoners in Germany. We were particularly struck with the appearance of the English prisoners, for they looked much worse than the others. Many of them were worn and thin, and some looked very ill. It would be hard to find a more dreary sight than these men presented, for they had been turned out of the German prisons in Belgium and had just managed to exist on the food given them by the Belgians – who doubtless had been obliged to go without food themselves in order to feed so many. We were very glad to have some bars of chocolate with us, which we had been keeping up to the time of the Armistice for the men in hospitals, and we broke them up and gave out all that we had in the mobile canteen.

Corporal Emily Rumbold
Women's Army Auxiliary Corps

After the Armistice, we were allowed to go to see the battlefields, and I went twice to Ypres. It was terrible. There was only one house left standing in the city – and that belonged to the chief of police. His was the only house that was not shattered. Of the Cloth Hall there were only ruins left.

There was utter devastation everywhere. The trees were smashed with just stumps left, about knee high. We stood on Passchendaele Ridge and looked across all this terrible destruction. How any man came out alive I can not imagine. The worst was the area around Ypres. There was devastation for miles around – it was very flat country and that was all you could see. We took a picnic lunch and we ate it with our feet in a shell hole. We saw the trenches too – the German ones and our own. The

German trenches were marvellous – quite different from ours. They were dug deeper and they even had electric lights.

Anonymous British officer, 1919

Yesterday I visited the battlefield of last year. The place was scarcely recognisable. Instead of a wilderness of ground torn up by shell, a perfect desolation of earth without a sign of vegetation, the ground was a garden of wild flowers and tall grasses. Nature had certainly hidden the ghastly scene under a veil of many colours. I was specially struck by a cross to an unknown British warrior which stood like a sentinel over the vast cemetery of the fallen in last year's battle, now hidden under the dense vegetation. Most remarkable of all was the appearance of many thousands of white butterflies which fluttered round this solitary grave. You can have no conception of the strange sensation that this host of little fluttering creatures gave me. It was as if the souls of the dead soldiers had come to haunt the spot where so many fell. It was so eerie to see them – the only living things in that wilderness of flowers. And the silence! Not a sound, not even the rustling of a breeze through the grass. It was so still that it seemed as if one could almost hear the beat of the butterflies' wings. Indeed, there was nothing to disturb the eternal slumber of this unknown who was sleeping his last sleep where he fell. A contrast indeed to the hideous crash of battle of a short year ago.

Gunner Harold Coulter
Royal Field Artillery
(on a battlefield tour in 1927)

It has been a terrible disappointment. The war is gone for ever – only a memory now. What we last saw as a vast desert of shell holes, bare tree stumps, mud, filth, smashed guns and tanks and dead men, is all waving cornfield, pretty gardens, brand new villages, noisy *estaminets*, charabancs, quarrelling children, and flighty girls. It makes one's heart thump. The only things left to remind one that memories once were immense realities are the cemeteries and the poppies.

Corporal Clifford Lane
2nd Battalion, Bedford and Hertfordshire Regiment

In 1920 I took my wife out to Belgium soon after we were married. We stayed for a week at the Chateau de Croix Dieux, and went out to find the grave of her brother, but in doing so we found that it was still dangerous to travel across fields because there were still bombs, shells and all sorts of explosives lying about. Every now and again there would be an explosion as the Belgian army destroyed live shells. Here and there people would shout to us, 'Stop! Don't come any further!' I thought, 'to hell with this – I'm not going to risk my wife's life and my own life again,' so we stopped exploring.

The countryside all around was devastated. It's hard to describe the brown tortured earth, the trees in the fighting areas reduced to stumps. Whole forests and woodlands were devastated and all the trees destroyed, they were knocked off, cut off, blown off – so that in places like Thiepval, which had been on the edge of woodlands, the woods were no longer there. They were simply an upheaval of clay and tree stumps. You could never imagine there had been a wood that would have blossomed when we first went out there. It had all been destroyed with the years of bombardment and attacks. It was simply like a wasteland – a desolate wasteland.

Vera Brittain
Author of Testament of Youth

Today, tours of the battlefields in France are arranged by numerous agencies; graves are visited in parties, and a regular trade has been established in wreaths and photographs and cemeteries. But that level of civilization had not been reached in 1921, so Winifred and I hired a car in Amiens, and plunged through a series of shell-racked roads between the grotesque trunks of skeleton trees, with their stripped, shattered branches still pointing to heaven in grim protest against man's ruthless cruelty to nature as well as man. Along the road, at intervals, white placards were erected in front of tumbledown groups of roofless, windowless houses; were these really the places that we had mentioned with gasping breath at Étaples three and a half years ago? I asked myself incredulously, as with chill excitement I read their names: Bapaume, Clery, Villers, Bretonneux, Peronne, Grivesne, Hedauville . . .

At Albert a circumspect row of Army huts, occupied by reconstruction workers, stood side by side with the humped ruin which had once been the ornate Basilica, crowned by its golden Virgin holding her Child aloft from the steeple. Was this, I wondered, apart from the huts, the place as Edward had known it?

As the car drove through the village to the cemetery, I realized with a shock from its resemblance to a photograph in my possession, that the grey chateau half hidden by tall, drooping trees had once been the Casualty Clearing Station where Roland had drifted forlornly and unconsciously into death. We found the cemetery, as Edward had described it, on the top of a hill where two roads joined; the afternoon was bright and sunny and just beyond the encircling wall a thin row of elms made a delicate pattern against the tranquil sky. The graves, each with its little garden in front, resembled a number of flower-beds planted at intervals in the smooth, wide lawn, which lay so placidly beneath the long shadow of the slender memorial cross. As I walked up the paved path where Edward had stood in April 1916, and looked at the trim, ordered burial-ground and the open, urbane country, I thought how different it all was from the grey twilight of the Asiago Plateau (where my brother Edward was buried), with its deep, sinister silence. The strange irony which had determined the fates of Roland and Edward seemed to persist even after death; the impetuous warrior slept calmly in this peaceful, complacent earth with its suave covering of velvet lawn; the serene musician lay on the dark summit of a grim, far-off mountain.

I left Louvencourt, as I thought, unperturbed; I had read the inscription on Roland's grave and gathered a bronze marigold to keep in my diary without any conscious feeling of emotion. Whatever, I decided, might be true of 1918, I was beginning to forget the early years of the war, and to recover from the anguish of its second Christmas. But late that night, back in the Paris hotel, I picked a quarrel with Winifred over some futile trifle and went to bed in a fury of tears.

Private George Morgan
West Yorkshire Regiment

When I go back there I feel I'm on consecrated ground. That ground has been trod by all those lovely lads who never came back. I think of that poem:

'They shall grow not old, as we that are left grow old: Age shall not weary them, nor the years condemn. At the going down of the sun and in the morning, We will remember them.'

I think it's marvellous. Because that's just how it is. You imagine them as they were then – not as they would be now – young, and in their prime, and never grown old.

Dolly Shepherd
Women's Army Auxiliary Corps

Following the Armistice there were a lot of troops in Calais waiting to be demobilized. The Germans let the prisoners loose, and some of them were making their way towards the coast, their feet bleeding and in a terrible state. We had to go along and pick them up anywhere we found them, and drop them off in Calais. They had to have very careful treatment, because they had had no food for some time.

Sergeant Thorpe-Tracey
1/6th Battalion, London Regiment

When I heard the war was over, I was disappointed. I wanted to have active service as an officer, but that was denied me. At the back of my mind I was glad, but the thought of what I missed out on did enter my mind.

I was in charge of recreational training in a place quite close to Calais, and I was approached by a major, as to whether I would assist him in co-ordinating various phases of entertainment, which meant we would go from one battalion to another in different parts of the country, organising football matches and inter-divisional league matches in order to keep the troops from boredom. We'd form football teams in each battalion or company – and also introduced other sorts of recreation. The major recommended that I be made an acting captain, but that was barred by the authorities because I hadn't got the crossed swords qualification from the School of Physical Training. There was not much enthusiasm, and it was often very difficult to raise a team of eleven – even from a whole division. But it improved as time went on. It was a reaction from the war – now it was over, we didn't want to do any more soldiering. We wanted to get back to Blighty and civilization, and get out of the army.

Private Arthur Barrowclough
Duke of Wellington's Regiment

After war had finished, we were walking across fields, picking up rifles and bombs and anything else to do with war. Two of our lads came across some shells that had been primed but never fired. They got all these shells and picked them up. They were coming to the dump, when one of the shells slipped off his arm and hit the striking pin, and exploded. They were both killed. It was terrible – they were just doing a duty of cleaning the countryside for the French folk.

Brigadier General F.P. Crozier
Royal Irish Rifles
(from his diary)

Arriving at our hotel in Boulogne to spend the night, while at coffee in the lounge, after dinner, my eyes fall on Margot – the pretty waitress who had waited on the thousands of British officers during the past four years and nine months. She is crying. She is very upset. We call her over. She is very reticent – but at last, breaking down completely, she unburdens her heart. Her trouble is simple. She has loved and been loved by many British officers during the hectic days – we guessed as much. Money has come easily. Excitement triumphed over remorse. She kept going while she supported an aged mother. Then she really fell in love with a good-looking young British officer, the son of a noble house who, having slept with her on many occasions, promised to marry her. He had just jilted her. Hence the tears, the remorse –

the utter disillusionment. The glamour, excitement and prosperity of war have disappeared – only utter disappointment remains for this poor girl.

Next morning as we enter the lounge after breakfast, there is no Margot. She has joined the millions of war victims. Demented, prostrate with anguish, frightened of the future, alone, forgotten, ignored, and perhaps wounded in pride – with British officers leaving France daily in large numbers, and her real lover ignoring her frantic appeals – she blew out her brains with a German pistol once given her by a colonel.

Private William Gillman
2/2nd Battalion, London Regiment (Royal Fusiliers)

We finally wound up at a place called Basecles, about 40 kilometres from Valenciennes, where the regiment was to be billeted. We were sorted out and allocated our various places to live and we went to these until we reported for duty. The chap who owned the house where I was billeted was the local quarrier, and he had a fairly big, solid place – a good type of dwelling. He had a daughter and I am afraid we fell for each other – she was a lovely girl called Céline. We got very close – but nothing intimate, because they were very devout people. I went so far as to go into Valenciennes to get a ring for her – it was by way of an engagement, although it was youthful seriousness when you look back on it. The quarrier had business connections in England and he must have had them check up on me. The family found out that I lived in a humble place – just a two-up, two-down, with no front garden in a poorish part of east London. Apparently they got back a very bad report – and her father judged me by the place that I lived in. Her parents decided that I was not a suitable person and they made her write to me to return the ring. She was very upset and tearful about it, and I was in such a temper. It seemed so unfair to judge me. Funnily enough, if it hadn't been for that, and we had married, I would either have been the owner of a quarry, she being an only child, or she would have been the first lady of West Ham, because I became the mayor.

Gunner Harold Flood
Royal Field Artillery

I found myself back with my battery, which was now stationed at the edge of the village of St Jean Capel near Bailleul. The CO sent for me as he had done several times before. 'Flood,' he began, 'you now surely can't refuse promotion whatever reasons you had before for refusing.' I'd promised my mother I'd refuse promotion to officer, since they were always the first to be killed – but now I'd kept my promise to her, and I considered I had no reason to refuse now that the Armistice was signed.

The next man I saw was Lieutenant John Edward Campbell, a former master at the Dumbarton Academy. He set things out for me. 'The top brass in London have decreed that the old Army Schoolmaster lot are to be discontinued, and a new Educational Corps is to be formed. We are to make a start, filling in the troops' time with a bit of schoolwork. I have the job to start in our battery and I want you to help me.' I agreed without pausing to think what the outcome would be.

I was given a room to myself in some old outhouse in which we established a bit of a library. A divisional meeting was called at Bailleul and we unit representatives were given the details of what was to be the Royal Army Educational Corps, and ordered to make a start.

By this time, the men had one main thought – which was to be demobilized – so our start at preparing for the new educational regime met with a mixture of humour and grumbling.

Another job with which I had to contend was a small group of

German prisoners. Two of them were chopping wood one day and I asked what they thought about the Kaiser being killed by us, along with Hindenburg. The Bavarian smiled and said he didn't care – all he wanted was to get back to his wife and children. The Brandenburger was angry. He waved his chopper in the air, 'The Kaiser good! Hindenburg, NEIN!' I thought he was going to go for me with his axe.

Brigadier General F.P. Crozier
Royal Irish Rifles
(from his diary)

I am to travel to Brussels and Cologne – but before departure, I talk seriously with my colonels. 'The men have evidently gone woman-mad,' I say. 'The venereal sick-rate is mounting. Many women must be diseased. I hear the Germans let the diseased women out of prison the day we arrived. It was an offence for a French woman to give a German soldier venereal disease, for which she was locked up for the protection of the soldiers. As the army is now returning to England by degrees, it is essential that, so far as is possible, we protect the women at home by returning their men clean. You must lecture your men on the subject and provide every convenient and reliable means of protection and sterilization. I will see the Mayor about the detection of the women and their treatment and segregation.'

At Brussels it is an orgy of vice in which many British soldiers join. The high-class prostitutes of the German Army are taken over by the officers of the Allied forces – yet only one short month ago, nothing was too bad for a German, nothing too good for ourselves! I see a British corps commander, lost in the whirl of post-battle gaiety, accosted by a woman of easy virtue, to his great annoyance, in the lift of his hotel. Her chief claim to his attention, according to her views, is that she was the war-time mistress of a German general!

In the halls and dining rooms, these ladies line up as they did in the days of German occupation. The women are the same, only the men and their uniforms are different, while the constant procession of couples to bedrooms aloft is as sustained and regular as in the days of German domination. And what of Cologne? There the servant girls in hotels, half-starved, lacking the ordinary necessaries of life, and even unused to simple crusts, pick up the crumbs which fall from their masters' tables and sell their bodies for half-loaves of bread in order that they may take to the aged and young in their homes the staff of life.

Captain Tom Sherwood
(in a letter to his wife)

I had 150 cases of Spanish flu in the Regiment in thirty-four hours – and thirty deaths. The three doctors at the hospital struggled manfully – then they all went down with it and fresh cases occurring had to be dealt with in the barracks. By this time, half the British officers were down too. I was all right, so started a hospital for my men in the barracks – I had no Persian officers – all in bed – so up to the hospital I went for medicine and thermometers. For three days I struggled along, treating the poor beggars – then I collapsed. Simply had to give in. Went to bed, temp 104 degrees! Had just seven days of it, got up yesterday, am quite all right again – just a bit groggy on my pins.

I have one dreadfully bad bit of news for you. Dear old Carr on his way to India, got this flu in Sirjan. Pneumonia set in, and he died on the 26th. I can't believe it. It has been a shocking blow to me – we were more than brothers to each other, and how he used to talk of meeting you and Boy – almost the last thing he mentioned was the present for Boy he was going to send from

Bombay. And now he's gone. Oh, it's a terrible tragedy, to have lived through the war as he did, to have escaped death as he did in France – and then to be bowled over by Spanish flu in Sirjan!

Colonel Bennet, retired
Royal Engineers
(in letter dated 9 February 1919 to his son's senior officer, Royal Field Artillery)

My son wishes to let you know that he arrived home safely yesterday (Saturday) after five days travelling. Whether he wishes me to add that he arrived with a temperature of 104 and went straight to bed where he now lies, I don't know, but so it is – a sharp attack of 'flu, and no wonder after seven hours in an open cattle truck from 3.30 a.m. to 11.30 in a snow storm and then 24 hours on board ship from Dieppe to Tilbury with the men on deck all the time. I fancy he was not fit when he started and so was liable to catch the flu. I don't expect he will be fit to return at the end of his leave, but I know he will be anxious to get back as soon as the doctor allows. His temperature still keeps at 104 and he is rather restless, but I hope for an improvement tomorrow. The doctors have lots of practice with the epidemic.

(in a letter nine days later)
My son is still alive, but I fear cannot last much longer. He has had a terrible time of it the last ten days, his wandering mind constantly dwells on his battery, the horses, etc. He seems to be talking on the telephone: 'All right then, I will send up 82 pairs of horses and 82 men', etc. Constant oxygen, strychnine etc keep him alive, but as I said, it cannot continue.

(in a letter, 25 February)
My poor boy died this morning after seventeen days' suffering.

I am writing to The Times about it, as it is scandalous that so many valuable lives should be wasted by exposure in cattle trucks in the journeys home and out. His end was peaceful and he was more or less conscious all the time, but we could not hear what he said the last few days.

Sapper Arthur Halestrap
Royal Engineers

I became ill, and my corporal was very worried. He called the infantry corporal and the corporal called the sergeant. And he was worried, and the sergeant called a sergeant major. And the sergeant major called the major and the major said, 'Oh, I don't know where the nearest medical unit is and if I did, it wouldn't be in time. Fill him up with rum and let him take his chance. He's got Spanish flu.'

The flu was killing millions in the world at that time. So I remember being hoisted up on my seat, then sitting on the floor on a blanket – that was all. I remember taking rum and the next thing I remember was when I said to my corporal, 'Could I have a cup of tea?' and he said, 'My God, we thought you were dead. You've been completely away from us for three whole days.' Just like that – but from that moment I was better.

Corporal John Collins
No. 1 Cavalry Field Ambulance, RAMC

The cavalry were the advance guard of the army of occupation, and it was the cavalry who crossed the frontier first and dug the bridgeheads on the other side of the Rhine. We moved on every day, and crossed the frontier on the 1st December. After 12 November, we had no supplies up for five days, including the day after the Armistice – for the first time in the whole war we were let down because everybody was celebrating behind the line and had forgotten there was such a thing as a front-line army. I made enquiries of a cavalry regiment and the chap told me that it was just the same for them and that they were on their iron rations – last reserves – which lasted for five days until they got more supplies up. It was bully beef, dog biscuits and water.

The trouble was that at this time influenza, which was really a bubonic plague, had started to spread through the world, and some good men who had lasted most of the war died through not being able to get better rations. Also, the men went into civilian houses, drank all the wine they could lay their hands on, and had their resistance lowered, so when they were attacked by the plague, in two days they were dead. We lost four men in the field ambulance – they were athletic men, taken ill in the evening, and dead the next day. I never caught it – I had great belief in my own strength. There was no preventative measure possible against this influenza. It was a virus and it killed more people throughout the world than were killed in the war. It was even caught on ships at sea.

The civilian population of Belgium was very quiet – there were no flag-waving turnouts, they just welcomed us. They were so far behind the battle lines there that it hadn't changed their lives a lot. They were agricultural people, and from seed-time to harvest for them was just the same as if there hadn't been a war – they had to carry on their lives.

Trooper Allan Hargreaves
Royal Field Artillery

We'd just got into Belgium when the flu struck us – and the ambulances were lining up every day taking people into hospital – but there was nobody coming back. We kept hearing that so and so had died – we didn't get a single one of them back from hospital. It was all over if you went into hospital. Our Sergeant Major got word from home that one of his daughters had died of the flu, so he got compassionate leave and went home. That was the last we saw of him. We heard tell a week or two after that while he was home, all his six children died of it, and his wife as well. He set off to come back to us, landed at the base, and then he too died.

I was the last to get it in our lot – and I thought I was going to miss it. But the Quartermaster Sergeant gave me a good tot of rum and rolled me in a blanket. I was all right the day after, although I was very weak for a day or so. It didn't last long – it would either kill you, or just go. The ones that went into hospital, we were hearing the day afterwards that they'd died. It would kill you in twenty-four hours – two days at most. That's when they started refusing to go into hospital. I know we lost more men from flu, day for day, than we did during the war. There wasn't a single man lost who stopped at the battery.

It was indescribable – you knew you'd finished with war – that you'd never see any more fighting – or you thought you wouldn't. I said to myself that once I got back I was going to get out of the army, and they'd never get me back in again – unless it was in Great Britain. I was not going overseas again to fight anybody's wars.

I was in a really bad state after the war, and I had a bout of shingles, and carbuncles, and a doctor who saw me asked me if I'd been ill at all during the war. I told him I hadn't, and he said, 'Then you're getting your share now!'

I used to dream that I was back in it again, and this went on for a good twelve months. But when I was out in France, when I did get a bit of sleep, I used to dream I was back home – and now it was the other way round.

Nurse Rosaleen Cooper
Voluntary Aid Detachment, sister of Robert Graves

There was a terribly infectious pneumonia epidemic that developed among the troops, so that I didn't get back home until well into the spring of March or April 1919. We were nursing some desperately ill men – some of them had been all through the fighting at the Front and escaped death – then died like flies in this epidemic. Great big, beefy guardsmen were struck down, and it seemed as if the germs preferred them to the wizened little Cockneys, and they died like flies. Only after that was over was I able to come back. It seemed to me rather a useless life then, just teaching little girls to play the piano after what I had been through. The whole experience of the war had a lasting and dramatic effect on my life.

Beryl Hutchinson
First Aid Nursing Yeomanry

After the Armistice, the Red Cross and army authorities were very keen for the nurses who had been in the Belone area to go and have a look at the battlefields. We went round with one infantry officer, one HQ officer, and a gunner. We took these three men round the battlefield, stopping at frequent intervals for them to tell us what had happened there. It was amazing how often the HQ men would say, 'But you went on from there – you didn't do as you were told.' The infantry men would argue with him. 'But we'd made arrangements about the barrage – everything was organized – if you'd only done as you were told, you wouldn't have lost so many men.' And so on – the men arguing. We went up to Ypres, and on to Hill 60, on that awful road across nowhere, which eventually led to Lille. Then we went to the Somme – it was just a field ploughed by a mad ploughman. Water, water

everywhere, and this awful turned soil. There was nothing you could say about anything that had happened there.

The nurses arrived as a merry laughing crowd for a day off, and they came back, they may have been hungry, but they came back a very chastened collection of women, who had at last seen the mud, and what a trench looked like. They were awfully grateful, because it gave them an insight into what their patients had been subjected to.

Nora Baker

Women's Army Auxiliary Corps

At the Abbeville cemetery, where I worked as a gardener, we had runners come up every afternoon from the various hospitals in the area, with notes to say how many burials there would need to be the next morning. The French people looked upon us with horror – oh it was dreadful. It was hard work – you have no idea! The soil there was only about two feet deep, but the rest was pure chalk. When it was frosty it was like walking on porridge. The graves that were already finished had to be two-thirds grassed over, then the other part where the cross was we had to plant trees and shrubs. It didn't help that we were very badly equipped with tools – the shears were very poor, so I cultivated an acquaintance with an army man who was able to sharpen them.

At Wimereux we had a wooden shed at the top of the cemetery with stacks of wooden crosses which we would put the names on. In Abbeville there was a problem because they were so short of ground there were two to a grave. When the Commonwealth War Graves Commission came into operation, there would be a makeshift wooden marker on the graves. The hospital messengers would leave the information with the plain wood coffins. The bodies were buried as quickly as possible. There was no special

service – we simply had to stand to attention while the padre officiated.

Mary Wilkinson
First Aid Nursing Yeomanry

The War Graves Commission asked us for drivers – although it was after we were demobilized – and several of us volunteered. I was quite pleased to stay out in France for a bit longer. I worked as a driver taking the gardeners round as they were making up the cemeteries, and we used to go to collect things from the ports. We used to travel all over the battlefields, because the Labour Corps men were going over the battlefields and collecting up the bodies and identifying them. They used to put up a screen where they were working, then take them to these wonderful cemeteries. The War Graves Commission did wonderful work, bringing these gardeners out – they lived in camps set up for them, and some settled out there.

Annie May Martin
Women's Army Auxiliary Corps

I was in France for nine months after the war, and we had more contact with the Americans. The thing that struck us most then, was that they thought they'd come over and won the war. I went on a tour of the battlefields with a mixed crowd, including some Americans – and everywhere the Americans said that this was where *they* won so and so.

I applied for some leave, and got permission to go to Paris for a week, and it was at the time when all the Allied generals attended the big peace parade. After the war, life was much more relaxed and we got about more. On one occasion we had a week's holiday and we got permission to go to the South of France. We noticed how untouched by the war the South of France was – life seemed to have gone on very much as usual. We went once to the grand opera, and as we came down the steps of the opera house, everyone in the building lined up to see my friend and me walking down the staircase – they'd never seen women in uniform before.

Sergeant Stewart Jordan

1/14th Battalion, London Regiment

After the Armistice we were staying in a village near Mons, and after a while passes were issued to those who wanted them to go to places like Paris for a few days for a break, so I thought it would be a good plan to see whether I could get a pass and go to Aachen in Germany. I wanted to see if I could locate my brother's grave. He had been wounded and taken prisoner, but died in hospital and been buried in Aachen.

I got to Aachen and found that the French were in occupation there, so I saw one of their officers and he got a billet for me. Then I was very fortunate to find a young woman who spoke perfect English, who was a great help and made all sorts of enquiries. Through her I found where my brother was buried. I went to the cemetery and located the grave, and found there were a few French soldiers there, looking for the graves of friends. They were making wooden crosses to put up over their graves, so I asked them if they would be good enough to make one for my brother's grave. They said they would, and I gave them a ridiculous amount of text to put on it. When I got back to Aachen, I went to the station and discovered that the regiment had already gone through Aachen, and they were already occupying a little town called Hilden, a few miles over the Rhine near Cologne.

I went on, found the battalion and told the colonel what I had been doing and he immediately said, 'We will get our carpenters to make a decent cross for your brother.' They made a very fine cross and painted it white with black lettering on it. Then I thought it would be nice if I could find a wreath of flowers to put on it, so I scouted around and found a little florist who said he had no fresh flowers, but that he could make a wreath with artificial ones. I said that would be better still, because they would last. He made me a huge wreath and put it in a big cardboard box – and wouldn't accept any money for it.

I got another pass to go back to Aachen and took the cross and the wreath with me. I found my way up to the grave, and the French soldiers had been good as their word and they had put up a cross – which was rather a crude sort of a thing – however I fixed up the new cross and propped the wreath up against it. I wondered if I could possibly get a photograph taken of it to send back to the old people, so I made some enquiries in the town and found a young woman photographer who agreed to take a photograph. I told her I wanted six copies and asked her to post them to me at an address in Hilden. I paid her for the photos and the postage, and after a week or so a package arrived. It had obviously been opened and censored. However, when they saw that it was just photographs and nothing else they let it through. I was glad about that, as I was able to send one home to the old.

Mrs B. Brooke
Escort and guide

After the war there were so many widows and mothers, asking if they could come over to France. It all seemed so far away to them, and if they could just come to France, they would feel nearer and more in touch with their sons – and perhaps know a little more than they had been told before. There were one or two men still in hospital, but on the whole it wasn't that that brought the women over.

The chaplain, Reverend Mullineaux, had so many letters from widows and mothers; he thought he must do something, so he replied to all their letters. He told them that if they could find their way to London, to Victoria Station, he would be responsible for getting them to France then bringing them back again. Then he wrote round to those of us who could speak French – which proved absolutely essential.

The chaplain took any place he could find which still had a roof on – that's what it came to, as there was such total destruction all round us – ruins. He didn't have to find the money for this himself – the women paid for everything. He simply had to organize it all for them. Part of my job was to hire taxis to pick these people up at the station – by this time the trains were running again – and then I had to arrange to take them to whichever hospital – or more generally the cemetery – they wanted to go to.

The people coming over were the widows and bereaved mothers. For a start, there was nowhere for them to go. They couldn't have found anywhere to stay. In small towns such as Albert or Cambrai there wasn't a roof left on the houses. You couldn't go anywhere and stay a night without someone with local knowledge to help you. In that respect, having our 'safe' house to go to was unique.

This was 1920, and I was there very nearly a year. Sometimes he got me to go down to Calais, which was his headquarters – where I'd meet the English boat every day, whether people were due out or not. It was just good that we were there, ready to help any English who looked a bit stranded.

We weren't with the Toc H organization. The chaplain called us the 'St Barnabas Mission', and we worked entirely with the war bereaved, who came from New Zealand, Canada and Australia.

I've never met anybody as tied up with the colonials as he was. He was such a staunch New Zealander himself, and I suppose that's why these people wrote to him. The women who came out were a very mixed lot, but it was very much down to who could afford to make the journey. If they went back having planted something on the plot, or having been able to pick something and take it away with them, it made all the difference. I know that by the letters they wrote me after they got home. They said that for me it was my work, but that I could have no idea what a help it was to them. They were really grateful – but what had they got out of it except the feeling that in future they'd be able to picture where their son or husband lay? The headstones weren't up then, so it looks quite different now.

The War Graves Commission did wonderful work and was a great help to some of the older men, as I saw at Étaples. These were older men who'd joined up because they felt they ought to – but were really too old. One man whom I got to know had come down from the line, passed as not A1 fit – and they kept him on, working at the cemetery in Étaples. There's a very big cemetery there, and on my days off, or if I had an hour or two to spare, I used to enjoy going up there and gardening in the cemetery. There was much more work there than he could handle, and I liked to help. I was so sorry for this man. I felt he was too old to be doing this work, but he went home once on leave and found that his wife had taken up with the lodger and he wasn't wanted any more, so when he returned, he said, 'I'm here for life now. I'm not going back to England.' I think he must have died soon after that – it was typical of the tragic events that happened, just on the side lines, as it were.

I worked many hours there at the Étaples cemetery, but after about a year, the flow of colonial widows dwindled, so the whole mission was stood down, and when I left my little house I effectively finished with everything to do with the war.

I didn't keep any tally of the number of people that came out with us over the course of the year, but it did amount to quite a few, although I could take no more than two at a time. But it was very personal for them, and I was with them all the time when they were there. There was no-one else for them to talk to.

It was always interesting for me to meet them, because they came from another country altogether – and it was work that was really needed, albeit in a small way. I never heard of any other country doing that. It was just lucky that the padre recognized the need and knew people he could call on who had had the experience to help.

They were extraordinary times in France and it wasn't a normal life. Everything was extraordinary, right from the time these people stepped off the boat. How could people arrive in France without being able to speak a word of the language? I was astonished that they came at all.

POST-WAR GERMANY

Following the signing of the Armistice, and before the signing of the Treaty of Versailles, three Allied armies, British, French and American, crossed the frontier into Germany as an occupying force. They found a mixed reception from the German population. Some were surprisingly unhostile – not so much bitter at their defeat, but relieved at the end of the fighting. What was apparent was the lack of even the most basic foodstuffs and materials to which the war had reduced much of the population.

Captain Herbert Sulzbach
German Artillery Officer

The war is over ... How we looked forward to this moment – how we used to picture it as the most splendid event of our lives

... and here we are now, humbled, our souls torn and bleeding, and know that we've surrendered. Germany has surrendered to the Entente!

In spite of it all, we can be proud of the performance we have put up, and we shall always be proud of it. Never before has a nation – a single army – had the whole world against it and stood its ground against such overwhelming odds. Had it been the other way round, this heroic performance could never have been achieved by any other nation. We protected our homeland from her enemies – they never pushed as far as German territory.

Unteroffizier Frederick Meisel
371st Infantry Regiment, 43rd Ersatz Brigade 10th Ersatz Division

Back to the Rhine – back, back without a stop. The highways were crammed with moving men – endless lines of men, war equipment, guns, pack trains, lorries and horses. Through France and Belgium, the grey columns moved. Nobody knew what the future held, but everybody's mind formed a belief in better days to come. Back to build up what was wrecked; back to a country proud, even in defeat. We crossed the border and were again on German soil. Our road took us over German fields, through German villages and towns. Flags were out in the buildings and signs decorated with late autumn flowers carried the inscriptions, 'Welcome Home'. German faces greeted us smilingly, blond and blue-eyed girls waved their handkerchiefs in glee, boys ran alongside us, eager to carry our rifles or equipment. Speeches were made and through it all, the church bells chimed, 'Peace at Last'.

Leutnant Fritz Nagel
18th Reserve Field Artillery Regiment

On 22 November we reached the Rhine Bridge near Kaiserlautern. Dirty and sloppy-looking revolutionary soldiers wearing red armbands stopped us and refused to let us cross the bridge. They feared our guns, as well as the thought that our whole outfit would join the counter-revolutionary army rumoured to be forming beyond the Rhine. They were quite orderly and polite, but I really did not care what happened to the guns. According to the Armistice conditions, the guns were to be surrendered and turned over officially to the French or Armistice commissions at some assembly point. I agreed to let these men have the guns against proper receipt for two motorized flak guns, two trucks and one passenger automobile. After these formalities were over, we parked the vehicles on the west side of the bridge. I shook hands with every man and dismissed them with instructions to get home the best way they could. That was the end of the war for me.

Princess Evelyn Blücher
Englishwoman married to a German aristocrat, living in Berlin

Among the aristocracy the grief at the breakdown of their country, more than at the personal fall of the Kaiser, is quite heart-rending to see. I have seen some of our friends – strong men – sit down and sob at the news, while others seemed to shrink to half their size and were struck dumb with pain.

I must confess that I myself feel shocked and surprised at the universal rejoicing manifested at the abdication of the Kaiser. They could not be more jubilant if they had won the war! *Vox populi, vox dei!* He may deserve his fate, but it seems very hard and cruel to throw stones at him at such a moment, when he must be enduring untold anguish and sorrow.

I never felt so deeply for the German people as I do now, when I see them bravely and persistently trying to redress the wrongs of the war, for which they were in truth never responsible. The greater part of them were men fighting blindly to guard an ideal – the *Heimat* – some patch of mother earth, a small cottage half hidden in its sheltering fruit trees, ploughed fields rising on the slope of a hill up to the dark forest of pines, maybe, or a wide stretch of flat country where the golden cornfields sway and wave in the wind as far as the eye can reach. This everything, that meant 'home' to them, they were told was in danger, and this they went out to save.

Major Thomas Westmacott
Headquarters, 24th Division

Our infantry began to cross the Rhine at 9.15 am. So as to do things really well, the German police were told to ensure that no wheeled German traffic was allowed on the streets – and they obeyed their orders to the letter. There were big crowds of Germans looking on in spite of the rain, but they seemed more curious than anything. I saw one woman in tears, poor soul, but bar that it might have been almost an English crowd. General Jacobs, my corps commander, stood under the Union Jack by a big statue of the Kaiser and took the salute. The men marched with fixed bayonets, wearing their steel helmets and carrying their packs, each man making the most of himself, full of pride and élan. Then came the guns, turned out as our gunners always turn themselves out. Mind you, the division was fighting hard all through the last battle, and they had been marching steadily through Belgium and Germany for the last thirty days, but the horses were all fit and hard as nails, and the buckles of the harness were burnished like silver. The mules were as fit as the horses and went by waggling their old ears as if they crossed the Rhine every day of the week. A German onlooker observed that the division must have just come fresh from England. It is difficult to remember what we were like last March and April, during the retreat of the Fifth Army – and to find ourselves now, as conquerors in one of the proudest cities in Germany.

Guardsman Fen Noakes
(in letter home, 18 December 1918)

I woke up just in time for crossing the German frontier, at the goal of all our hopes. We stopped at Aachen (Aix-la-Chapelle), a large junction for the old Paris-Berlin-Petrograd expresses, and again at Düren. When we got to Cologne we detrained and waited for three hours on the platform. Then might be seen how the Guards invaded Germany and fried bacon in Cologne Station, for we made fires and cooked our supper. At last we moved off and entered Cologne singing 'Good-bye-ee' – the song that has taken the place of 'Tipperary' in the army now. It was a great moment! At last, the goal of our ambitions is reached, and our victory is demonstrated. The Rhine – *der Deutscher Rhein* – is now guarded by British troops and the Union Jack flies over Cologne. Instead of the Kaiser eating his Christmas dinner in London, we shall eat ours in the heart of Germany. What a change!

The inhabitants do not seem at all hostile – indeed, I was greatly surprised at the pleasant manner in which we were received. They are not enthusiastic – one could not expect it – but they are very polite and seem anxious to please us. In the shops they serve us with many smiles and are strictly honest in changing French or English money. The language does not present such a difficulty as in France, owing to the similarity between German and English, and, also, many of the Germans speak English quite well.

Captain Charles Wilson
1st Battalion, Gloucestershire Regiment

Our only concern was to find something to drink to celebrate, but there wasn't a thing to be had – not a bottle of wine or anything. We marched on the 12th of November for Germany, as part of the army of occupation. The Germans at first were very sullen. We marched into the villages where we were to be billeted and all the shutters were up – there was nobody to be seen, like a dead village – but then the children started to come out, and the troops started playing with them and giving them chocolate. Then the women thought perhaps we were not so bad after all, and the shutters came down. We were billeted on them in their houses, so they had to get used to us, but the German men were very sullen. They were working in their fields in their field grey uniform, and we never saw them. They'd taken their uniforms home with them.

The atmosphere was of a completely defeated country, and they were dreadfully short of materials. There was no rubber – my batman was cleaning my trench boots with rubber soles, and the locals were gasping in wonder at this. They had no rubber for their bicycle tyres.

Corporal John Collins
No. 1 Cavalry Field Ambulance, RAMC

We crossed the frontier on 1 December 1918, rather to the north. The first thing I saw was a man in German uniform, who walked up to the door of a house in the street. It was opened by a woman who closed it again. He knocked again and she opened it, and she had an axe in her hand. There were no laurels for the defeated army there. She was evidently one of those Amazons who were determined to give no welcome to their defeated husbands. It caused some amusement, and we thought, 'thank goodness the English women are not like that!'

Elsewhere I noticed German civilians put up an enormous display of welcome for their own troops, with placards and displays at every railway station and in every town – and they were welcoming home their own defeated army – but they just accepted us. They thought that we were going to do much more plundering – but in fact there wasn't any and we brought our own rations with us. They unfortunately had none to spare, they were very short of food. They were at worst quite indifferent to us, but in some places, even quite warm. I never had any difficulty in getting what I wanted if it was available, and would not cause deprivation to the German people.

The Allies allowed the ex-German soldiers in civilian clothes to form the equivalent of the British Legion, and they did that for political purposes. Germany was rife with Bolshevism and Communism at the end of the war, and it was decided that the men who got home should be allowed to join ex-comrades associations. They had a march with a band through the village we were billeted in and we took no notice – they were even doing the goose-step – but we still took no notice. They were ex-soldiers getting together, the same as the British Legion would have. This was an old comrades association – not an aggressive body – although years later it turned that way.

As we crossed over the Rhine at Bonn, the salute was taken by General Sir Arthur Curry, the commander in chief of the Canadian forces. In England at the time there was a popular song, 'When we wind up the watch on the Rhine', and there were all the troops winding up their watches, crossing over the bridge as they went. I had no watch, but it made me laugh, because they were all simple fellows and they were winding up their watches.

Gunner Harold Flood
Royal Field Artillery

The order came for us to move up to Siegburg in Germany, which was the chosen place for us to stand to in case the peace treaty was not signed.

One day I went into a shop attended by a young German woman, and I casually remarked, 'Are you glad the Armistice has been signed and hope the Peace Treaty will soon be signed?' Her face saddened with her reply. 'I don't care what happens. All I know is my only brother has been killed in this beastly war.' That shook me, 'I am sorry,' I said, and I left the shop in a chastened mood.

On another occasion I was ordered to take a wagonload of men for a day's outing in Cologne. When we arrived, I turned the men loose and, being a church-going man, I was naturally attracted by the Cathedral. Inside I stood gazing round, and presently noticed a German in uniform, divested of numerals, which showed him to be a demobilized soldier. He strolled towards me and in my small smattering of German, I asked if he spoke English. He replied that he did.

After my remarking on the beautiful building and the good fortune for them in its having missed the attention of the enemy, he got round to what he really wanted to tell me. 'You English have not really won the war.' At once I interrupted him. 'Come outside – this is not the place for such conversation.'

Outside I told him to continue. He said that peace was being arranged by our socialists and theirs.

'When were you active with the forces?' I asked. 'Six months ago,' came his answer. 'What a pity,' I said. 'Do you know the firing range of our 18–pounder guns?' He said he did, so I informed him of our being unable to fire six rounds without limbering up and going forward.

'You were running like rabbits. Now understand this. I do not blame your womenfolk and elderly people welcoming you back across the Rhine with flowers, but take it from me, the time will come when we English will regret having been prevented from crossing the Rhine into your country to show the people we really *had* won the war.'

With that, we had had enough of this discussion and I invited him to join me in a restaurant across the square from the Cathedral – to which he agreed. On entering, he gazed round at the customers already in the place. With a horrified look he turned to me and said it was not possible as there were officers present. Anger welled up in me and I burst out, 'Damn you! Sit down. You are my guest, officers present or not. They are just customers like ourselves.' He obeyed me and sat down. I ordered coffee and some pastries and we enjoyed a conversation on more general – and happier – topics. We left the restaurant in a happy mood and said goodbye, wishing each other good luck.

Sergeant Stewart Jordan
1/14th Battalion, London Regiment

I settled down in Hilden and took charge of the officer's mess. At first I was billeted over a butcher's shop, and the butcher himself had been in the Prussian Guards. He was a great big tall fellow, and he still used to wear his Guards' cap. When I used to come in of an evening, around ten o' clock, he used to be standing behind the counter, sharpening his knives.

There was no animosity towards the British whatsoever. I hadn't been there very long when we took over a very large old house – a lovely place. I had a bedroom there, with a four-poster bed, a duvet and central heating – in those days, in 1919! There was a large room downstairs which was used for the officers' meals and there was a very nice kitchen.

I remained in charge there until I was demobbed. My duties

were to see that the place was run properly – the meals were part of the army rations but I supplemented those with various things that I was able to buy from the shops in Hilden – fresh vegetables, fruit – and sauerkraut, which the officers rather liked. I arranged with the cook about catering for parties, and organized my staff – there were waiters, and the officers all had their batmen, and I had an engineer to look after the boiler.

We used to have a case of whiskey and a case of port sent out from London about once a month, and I could buy other drinks from the village if the men wanted them and paid a subscription. I generally ran the mess in the manner of a small hotel. The officers all seemed very pleased and everything went very smoothly.

The officers all behaved very well – they had to, especially in front of the Germans! We had to be absolutely spick and span. On the whole, their drinking was quite abstemious – I don't think the colonel would have allowed any bad behaviour. The colonel was a regular – a great disciplinarian but he was absolutely fair, and I had tremendous respect for him. When I told him that I had located my brother's grave, he couldn't have been nicer about it.

The colonel received a request from my old firm 'Huntley and Palmers' asking if I could be demobbed as soon as possible as they had a job waiting for me, so with his help I think I was demobbed rather earlier than I would have been otherwise.

Louie Johnson
Voluntary Aid Detachment

I was still not demobilized at the end of 1918, so I asked if I could be released as soon as possible to join my husband, who went with the troops into Germany. There was no hope of being demobilized by Christmas – in fact I was told it would be at least six months.

My husband wrote to say they had permission for one or two of them to have their wives join them – generally there was no accommodation for wives. He'd got permission for me to go, so he sent me details as to how I was to get to Cologne – it was all rather terrifying. I was to cross the Channel to Ostend, then get the train to Cologne. My husband was with a field ambulance unit about four miles outside the city, but fate stepped in at Ostend, and there he was on the deck! I've never been so grateful to see anybody in my life! We had a happy weekend in Brussels, then went on to Mulheim.

Conditions in Germany were dreadful. My husband had a billet in a doctor's house and also living there were his wife, two sons and two brilliant daughters. They spoke five languages and that shattered me! It made me feel like a little worm! Their house was a tall building – full of professional people who were all very nice – but they were suffering acutely. The bread they had was definitely made from sawdust and bran. I never saw a butcher's shop the entire time I was there. They used to have a goose from time to time, which would smell to high heaven – they used to keep it down in the cellar. Every day outside our windows – which were not at pavement level – there would be up to a dozen children, calling out for food – for anything we could give them.

At first I didn't like to offer the family food, but I saw how they were suffering. They were not a military family, but they had lost a son in the war – one remaining son was a doctor and the other at university, so I said to the wife, 'I wish I could have some brown bread – I can only get white bread from the mess.' We used to get white bread from the mess, and a ration of meat every day for my husband, myself and his batman. She was very sceptical, and Maria, who spoke very good English, said, 'Mother doesn't think you mean that.' But I said I did. They watched suspiciously to see if I ate it – but I did. Our ration of meat for the three of us was more than we needed, and Maria used to cook it very nicely for us, and she had a kitchen maid who used to wait on us. I said to Maria, 'When we have had our dinner at night, we do not want that meat again. It's no use to us, and I don't want it cooked up for lunch the following day, as we will be out for lunch. Our batman brings in fresh every day.' So they more or less lived on our leftovers.

At Christmas I wrote home to my mother asking her to send me some wool to knit for them – and some mincemeat, as they'd never heard of mince pies. I had a knitted scarf, which I used to wear as I walked down Frankfurtstrasse. The children used to follow me and grab hold of this scarf. '*Wunderschön! Wolle!*' 'Wonderful! Real wool!' So I knitted them a scarf and gave it to Frau Meerbeck – and she was delighted. Then I went into their kitchen and asked if I could use the oven. I made them some mince pies for Christmas – and they liked them very much.

Every Friday night we were invited into their dining room to have dinner with them, and the effort they made was wonderful. They would bring out their crystal and silver and cook something in the meat line – then they'd serve a plum tart. They were very good to us. They were very short of food and one day there was great excitement when a relative from the country brought them two eggs – they were wild with excitement. They brought one in for me. 'Ein Ei, Frau Johnson!' An egg! They insisted on me having this egg, which was very kind.

CHAPTER 4

Demobilization

Although regular career soldiers who had survived the war had in prospect an ordered return to the UK, or possibly a direct posting to duties across the Empire, the enlisted men were in line for demobilization and a return to work at home. For most, that couldn't come too soon. The British Government put in place criteria for prioritizing who should be demobbed first – which proved both unpopular and, for those with influence, all too simple to circumvent. Stuck in camps with no proper duties to occupy them, the men often became restless and angry at the delay in being allowed home. Some became mutinous and their refusal to toe the line called down the full wrath of the military command to remind them of their status as soldiers.

Some waited months for permission to leave the military life behind. Swapping their uniforms for demob suits, Britain's servicemen came home and started looking at what the future held for them.

Gunner Leonard Ounsworth
Royal Garrison Artillery

We were kept occupied while we were waiting to be demobilized – we were playing football several times a week, and we had the horses to look after and exercise every morning. There were other activities – including a boxing tournament once a week. The system for demobilization seemed to be a fair one – they took out the essential people first. Regulars – the men who had done their time with the Colours, and of whom some had up to thirteen years' service – were the first out.

We had about twenty Welsh miners come to us – God knows why – and they caused a lot of trouble, because there had been a miners' strike in the latter part of the war and we in the army didn't think much of that. They arrived with us three weeks after the Armistice, but they had been recruited and in the pipeline at home, so the process had to go on and they were still bunged out to France. Useless! We chaps didn't agree with their having gone on strike while the war was on, interrupting munitions production. There was a lot of ill feeling about it at the time.

I was demobbed from Ripon, and the train came in – they'd stopped us getting two earlier trains for Leeds, and the RTO on the platform said that this was not the troop train – but that that would be along soon. We said we'd heard that one before, and all piled on to this train – but they wouldn't move off until everybody was back out on the platform. Somebody went to the driver and asked if he was going to drive the bloody train – or should we? He decided he should drive it. We came into Leeds, to this dead-end platform and there was a force of military police waiting for us on the other side of the big iron sliding gates. There were over two hundred blokes on the train, and they said, 'Here's a chance to get our own back on these buggers,' and they just climbed over those rails. The blue-uniformed railway police just put their hands behind their backs and strode off. I didn't have to get off because my forward train went out of the same bay, so I just sat and watched – and in less time than it takes to tell, there were all these MPs stretched out unconscious on the platform.

Major Richard Russell
Royal Field Artillery

Based at Dieppe, demobilization was a very slow business, with chaps going off just in ones and twos. It was not too bad when we still had horses because the chaps were kept busy in the stables, feeding and watering the horses and taking them out on parades. While we waited to be demobilized, we used to ride around the country, exploring everywhere, but then the day came when the horses had to go. That was very sad – I was fond of my two horses and I wondered whose hands they would fall into and where they were being taken. Not many horses were sent home to England, and I know a lot went with the men who were tasked with the occupation of Germany. Other horses were sold to the French.

As the demobilization process dragged on, it was a problem to keep chaps amused. We had daily parades and inspections but that was just about all we could do. We celebrated Christmas there, so we collected what money we could and laid on quite a good Christmas dinner for our chaps, with the usual visit from the divisional general and senior officer.

One thing we could do to pass the time was play football and we got a number of matches arranged – but it was still very hard to keep the chaps amused, when all they wanted to do was to go home. But they just had to wait. The demobilization process was fraught with difficulties – down at the base there were front-line fighting troops waiting to go home alongside the bakers, ordinance men, tailors and others who had never been on the Front at all. They were crying out to be demobilized, and had been expecting to get home quickly, because they had been out at the frontline for years.

There was one great source of rancour during demobilization – the white paper. Anybody who got hold of a white paper got absolute priority over everybody else. This special ticket was reserved for what they called 'key men'. These were people who had special knowledge or skills, who would be able to help get industry back on its feet. To my surprise, a boy of about eighteen turned up at the battery – and I'm damned if he didn't get a white paper! Apparently his father was a miller and he was considered indispensable to his father's business. That really was too much.

I knew that if I let this chap off before all the other lads who had been out at the Front for years, I'd be asking for trouble. I was very angry about the injustice of it – obviously his father had knobbled an MP to get this white paper. There was no other possible reason for it. So I did the only thing possible, and I tore up his paper and forgot about it. Not long after there was a big row in Parliament about the system and the white paper scheme was withdrawn all together. Eventually we were reduced to the minimum number of men and horses we needed to get the vehicles to the port.

General James Whitehead
Assistant Adjutant, General Headquarters, British Expeditionary Force

The scheme was based on the priority release of 'key' men needed to start up industry and such men received from home green cards, on receipt of which they were sent home. I soon heard rumours that things were not going well in this respect: two cases which I recollect being that a green card had been received for the release of the mace-bearer of a mayor and the other for the release of someone's butler. I arranged for the proper scrutiny of green cards and soon stopped that racket.

Lieutenant George Thomas
8th battalion, Sherwood Foresters
(in a letter to his parents)

Everyone is anxious to get home, and yesterday twenty-five coal-miners went from my company. But today I have two new officers join the company. I cannot in the name of common sense under-stand why they are sending people out from England now. Flocks of people are coming out who have been well dug in some job at home – there is nothing for them to do, either! I have now seven officers, and when we were fighting about a month ago, I had two.

I am quite fed up with the Army now. The job is finished and one put up with a great deal of things when there was a necessity to help beat the Boche, but now a lot of things simply irritate me. Nobody has as yet been demobilized except coalminers, and they are going as fast as the authorities can print new forms. There are extremely few men who have any desire to remain in the Army – all are anxious to discard their khaki now that the job is finished.

I trust you will all have a very merry Xmas – I fear there is no hope of my being there with you this time ... better luck next year.

Private Raynor Taylor
Welch Regiment

I had hoped for an early demob, but found myself posted to a unit guarding German prisoners before their repatriation. One Saturday four of us were off duty, walking down a country road. We were accosted by an elderly gentleman wearing a Norfolk suit – the type worn by country gentlemen, with a long, belted jacket and knickerbocker trousers, stocking and boots. I saw this man coming up the road and I remember bidding him the time of day. He asked what we were doing and where we came from, and he was very interested in everything we told him.

Suddenly he said, 'I wonder if you boys would like to have tea with me?' Well, imagine! Somebody offering you a civilized tea instead of what we were going back to. Of course, we accepted, so he turned and walked back the way he'd come and we went with him. He turned in at a big house, a fair distance from the road.

We went in and there was an elderly-looking woman there – he introduced us and said, 'we have four boys for tea.' Then he took us into a big room, and we sat down at a long table. As we sat talking, I noticed there were a lot of pictures around the room. We talked about what we did, where we had been and where we came from – then the lady came in and set out the tea things. We had thinly-cut bread and butter with jam and cakes – there was no limit to what we could eat! We really ate our fill, then we sat and chatted. By this time we had established a friendly relationship, and I was able to get up and have a look at the pictures around the room. In the main they were historical pictures – battle scenes and events – which I found very interesting. Above the fireplace was a lithograph – it was a print of a poem. I stood there and looked at it – I knew the poem and as I stood there, without realising, it, I was mouthing it, silently. Suddenly a voice said, 'Do you know it?' I said, 'Yes,' and he asked if I could recite it. The poem was called 'If'. It is still one of the best poems in the English language as far as I am concerned. The thing that I remember most was the line, 'If you can make one heap of all your winnings and risk it on one turn of pitch-and-toss, and lose, and start again at your beginnings and never breathe a word about your loss, and if you can fill the unforgiving minute with sixty seconds' worth of distance run, yours is the Earth and everything that is in it and – which is more – you'll be a Man my son.' I got to the end and he said, 'Very good! D'you like that?' I said I did, and he said, 'So do I – in fact I like it better now than the day I wrote it.' How about that? The man was Rudyard Kipling, and if I live to be a thousand I will never forget that day.

The fact that I had met Rudyard Kipling didn't really register with me. I didn't realise what an important man he was – until some time afterwards. There was that part of the poem – to 'Lose and start again at your beginnings ...' and I think back and realise that Rudyard Kipling never mentioned when we were there that he lost his only son in the war. That is quite something.

I believe the loss of his son at the end of the war altered Rudyard Kipling's whole life and character. Previously he was a great 'Empire' man – but after the loss of his son, and I think because of his age, he had no family and he became a bit of a recluse – which was sad because he was such a nice fellow. I feel he was living up to his own poem by not mentioning his son. He gave us a good meal – and he gave me something to remember for the rest of my life. (A GENTLEMAN)

Lance Corporal Bertram Neyland
Royal Engineers

After the Armistice it was more than a year before we were demobilized, and this delay, particularly among the volunteers and conscripts, caused some bitterness. Infantrymen were very anxious to get home to their families, but I must confess that we were having such a good time then, I wasn't in any hurry to be demobilized – not that I could do anything to influence it. I was playing rugby for the Westmoreland and Cumberland Yeomanry, and soccer for the Signals team, and it was a wonderful life.

They were marvellous times in Limerick, but there was a lot of trouble too between the Sinn Feiners and the police. I never saw any symptoms of this unrest – I was mixing with a signals bunch, people like ourselves, and I suppose most of us were rather enjoying the freedom of life once the tension of war had been removed. I was given a stripe – lance corporal – and was due for demob. In the summer of 1919 the call came. I went alone to Dublin, and when I got there I wondered why the other chaps hadn't been brought up too. But I found out there was a non-descript band of about thirty soldiers from various units. They were all going for demob and they wanted an NCO to lead them. I happened to be free so I was detailed to take them over to England. For me it was quite an experience, because I had never given a word of command in the army since I had been made Lance Corporal. I carted them around the parade ground and eventually down to docks and on to the ship. The following day we got to Bedford, where I handed over my draft to the authorities, who then removed my stripe because I was only 'acting'.

I expected to be sent to Maresfield in Sussex to be demobbed, but there was industrial trouble in Britain at that time and the authorities were expecting a national strike. So instead they sent me down to Salisbury. I got into the garrison football team and I thought about joining the evening classes in local schools. All that was threatened when an officer approached a group of us, and said, 'Look here chaps, you're all wireless signallers. How would you like to go to Russia?' Apparently Kerensky was trying to form a White Army to fight the Red Army, so we put our hands up. We'd had a wonderful respite in Ireland, and we knew what was waiting for us back in the Post Office. We knew it wasn't that much of a job, existing on about two pounds a week – and we knew that our postal service wouldn't be impaired by our remaining in the army, so four of us said we'd go.

Soon after that, the officer came back, 'You're a lot of swine, why didn't you tell me? I am not allowed to touch Post Office people. The sooner you get back to civilian life the better.' So my dream of going to Russia and having a few more months in the army slipped away.

Private Raynor Taylor
Welch Regiment

I got a posting on passport duty at Folkestone, that involved examining people who wanted to go to France. Naturally, France was a no-go-area for civilians in the war and there were a lot of people who had relatives and friends and business interests who wanted to go for personal reasons. These people had got to get a passport, and it was our job to examine these passports.

The passport office was at the train station, and we occupied the guard's hut. Anybody at the station would have to come through that office and we examined the passes for the vehicles and individuals.

We lined up along the dockside, and the crowds began to gather. A group of well-dressed people got off a train – people of note who were part of the welcoming party. The peace had been signed, and the British delegation was coming home on SS *Brighton*. They didn't seem able to bring this paddle steamer in, and it had to come in askew. Then when they wheeled the gangway up, some of these dignitaries went one way, and some another. The more I think about it, the more undignified it appeared. The senior members of the Cabinet were there to welcome Lloyd George, but the gangway would only take one at a time, and two of them were trying to get on it at once. I think it was a matter of protocol, and in a way it was very funny. One of the men was General Smuts, who had been co-opted into our War Cabinet.

Then there was a period of waiting. You could just imagine them all, having drinks and congratulating one another and saying what good lads they all were. Eventually, after what seemed quite a while, the party emerged. Lloyd George came out first. He was a commanding figure – small and stumpy with white hair and a white moustache. Everybody was cheering like mad as he walked down the gangway, where I was standing half way down, and when he got right opposite me he stopped. I was petrified – I didn't know what to do. I was wondering if I had committed some misdemeanour. But all he said to me was, 'Wonderful!' and he spoke in a very Welsh accent, 'Wonderful, wonderful, wonderful.' I didn't realise what he meant until later, when I found out it was because, as he passed me he saw my cap badge with its big Prince of Wales feathers – it was the cap badge of the Welch Regiment. When he saw it, he thought they had brought up a Welsh contingent to act as a guard of honour.

He asked me, 'What part of Wales do you come from, boy? I froze – I didn't know what to say, so I replied, 'I don't come from Wales, sir.' He laughed. 'You don't come from Wales? Don't come from Wales! Where **do** you come from?' I said, 'Near Manchester.' Strangely, I couldn't have said anything better, 'Manchester? Manchester? I was born there. Whereabouts in Manchester?' I explained that it wasn't so much Manchester as Oldham. 'Oh I have been to Oldham many times. I know Oldham.' He was parroting on, and the Cabinet was waiting behind him as he spoke to me for several minutes. Before he went, he pulled a photograph out of his pocket, about the size of a postcard, and he wrote on it 'David L George'. He tore it in two and he gave me half and said, 'Keep that, boy.' I believe he gave the other half to the girl who was the canteen manager, organizing the feeding of troops.

As they streamed off the gangways the men were all patting him on the back and the women were trying to get at him. My mates were all asking me what he said to me.

On another occasion we had a bunch of about twelve Australians coming in. That was a bit scary, because these men were all supposed to be under sentence of death – probably for desertion or perhaps murder.

During the crossing they had broken out of their cells and managed to get a hold of a rifle or two and you could hear them shooting at the smokestack. We were sent on duty on the dockside, and were issued with rifles and bayonets – we didn't normally have these. When the ship docked, these Aussies came off first.

I was at the gate when these Aussies came off, wearing their slouched hats, and swaggering as if they hadn't a care in the world. They'd evidently managed to get hold of a supply of drink while they were on board. I was hoping they didn't stop near me, because they walked off in ones and twos and they were joking with people – and with the guards. One fellow came over to me –

I was only very small and he was a massive man – and I stood there with my rifle at my side. He said, 'All right cobber, what you gonna do with that?' pointing at my rifle. I said, 'Oh I don't know' – and he took hold of it, and started shaking me about. I was pretty scared. While he was talking to me, these other fellows came out until about six were gathered around me. However, they moved on and were taken to the guard hut. Guards had been sent there from the nearby military camp at Shorncliffe to look after them. Look after them! They were there just one night, and they kicked the back out of the hut and walked off. There were enquiries made as to why no-one had tried to stop them – but nobody wanted to try.

Private Leonard Stagg
Royal Army Medical Corps

After the Armistice, the chaps got fed up. One day all I had to do was carry a table from the orderly room to a barn down the road, and the next day I had to carry it back again. There was nothing for us to do. There was a battery of Artillery, and they said that all they'd done since the Armistice was polish guns – so they said they weren't going to do it any more. It was pretty much a mutiny, and they sent a battalion of Australians there to arrest them. When the Australians arrived and heard what the trouble was, they threw their rifles down and joined them. There was a bit of devilment in them, but they were good fellows.

General James Whitehead
Assistant Adjutant, General Headquarters BEF

The slow rate of demobilization was being much criticized at home and the Prime Minister suddenly ordered that all men at home at that time were to be demobilized at once. This put fat into the fire, but they persisted with it in spite of the protests of the army authorities. The results were unfortunate. We had, with much pain, made elaborate arrangements in the BEF for those men last on the list for demobilization to be given that Christmas leave. Directly it became known that those men had been demobilized, mutinies were widespread, chiefly in the leave camps, among the men who had just returned from home leave, and therefore missed this demobilization.

One of the most serious incidents was at Calais, where there were several thousand men. They took charge and refused all orders. The Commander-in-Chief gave me full authority to interrogate the men and demobilize any hard cases on the spot. I motored at once to Calais with two of my officers, and having reached the camp and asked for the Commanding Officer, was told that he had been deposed. I said that if that was the case, it was of no use for us to remain, but we were told that we could not leave. I then met the 'delegates', to whom I spoke in no unmeasured terms. They then let us leave, but just at that moment, the camp was found to have been surrounded by a division, led personally by Lord Byng, and the trouble ended. The ringleaders were tried by court martial and several were sentenced to death – but these sentences were commuted to terms of penal servitude. A perfect example of the ill effects of a thoroughly bad order from on high.

Corporal Emily Rumbold
Women's Army Auxiliary Corps

There was a lot of unrest among the men about the way they were being demobilized. The men at the corps found they were not being demobilized in turn with the people up the line – although many of them were back because they had been wounded. They thought that they should be demobilized in due turn with the men up the line. Many still had to sleep on the ground – they didn't have any tents or huts. They had a lot of legitimate grievances.

One man started going round among the troops saying that something ought to be done about the situation – like a strike or other protest. I don't know exactly what the upshot was, but he was preaching sedition, and had the war still been on, he'd have been shot. Eventually he was arrested and taken to Boulogne where, rumour had it, he *was* going to be shot. That started off the rest of the troops – it wasn't so much a strike, as much as dissent. I think there were some 32,000 troops around the Calais area, and as the men came back from leave, their rifles were taken away from them. I seem to recall they were just kept in the camp.

Only a fence of barbed wire separated us from the ordinance men in the camp next to ours, and on one occasion the regimental sergeant major – whom they hated – got all the men out on parade. He gave the order – 'right turn' – and not a soul moved. One chap told us we should have seen the look on his face – he was horrified. Nobody had said a word about this mutiny beforehand – and certainly not to us girls, because they thought we'd only give the game away. They didn't do anything – they just stood.

After a day or two, some of us were going down to the depot as usual – we weren't going on strike. But the major told us we were to go back to our camp and not go to the depot, as there were a hundred men on patrol down there to turn away any girls who arrived to work. They were regarded as blacklegs, and they'd throw out any of us who went to work.

The official reaction was terrific. They sent for a general from up the line – an extremely nice man – to come to HQ. They had other VIPs there too, and once they heard about this general coming, the men got up a procession of 2000 and marched down to base HQ. The general agreed to meet a deputation from the procession – and he was extremely tactful and knew how to handle men. He said, 'You must go back to work – all go back to your duties, and I will see what I can do about it.' The general gave them two days to get back to work and he warned them that he would go round to every unit, and if they were not back at work, they would be fired on by troops. The deputation told the men what the general had said – and they took him at his word. They went back to work, and the general kept his word – but we still had machine gunners in our office, and they didn't leave until everybody was back at work. It was terribly serious.

Not only did the general keep his promise, he had the system for demobilization changed, so leave for the men was speeded up. He resolved the problem of the men's sleeping and living conditions too. The war was over and they said their depots were stacked with floorboards and things for the tents – so he commandeered these. He was very good – and the men were evidently satisfied, because all the unrest stopped.

Brigadier General F P Crozier
Royal Irish Rifles
(in his diary)

Realizing the trials and dangers of demobilization, I tighten up the discipline, arrive at a proper understanding with those who await their turn to cast off the war uniform, and provide counter attractions, so far as is possible, in order to avert the chaos which I feel sure will be the inevitable sequel to disappointment and disillusionment: for soldiers are but human and all cannot be demobilized at once. Elsewhere impatient men burn their camps and huts, assault their officers, imprison their generals, and the staffs, and hold up demobilization itself – the very thing they wish to speed up – by their mutinous conduct and the destruction of the demobilization papers. In one instance a British division is marched to Calais from Flanders to restore order.

The majority of the men are savage for freedom. Tactful handling of the problems is required and when this is the rule, the British soldier is, as usual, sensible.

Mutiny is the invariable outcome of official incompetence, and when the mutineers are punished, as must always be the case – for no mutiny can be condoned – responsible senior officers should invariably share a similar fate. This was not done in 1919.

Guardsman Horace Calvert
2nd Battalion, Grenadier Guards

I was going to the canteen and when I got there it had been raided! Other buildings were ransacked! They were going to attack the officers' mess! I saw staff officers surrounded by a lot of troops who were telling them they wanted money paid every week – they hadn't been paid for weeks. They wanted the right to go into Le Havre, and they wanted the Military Police easing up a bit on them. They shouted at them – one of them was a staff brigadier! I was on the outskirts and didn't join in. I just listened. I thought, 'I'm not getting mixed up in that lot.' The discipline I'd received was that you accept orders without question. I knew that these men were trying to make their demands in an improper way. There were two or three ringleaders who were doing all the talking and waving everyone around to come and join them, and there were two or three hundred there. It wasn't a mutiny – I would merely call it a disturbance. The officers managed to disperse them eventually. They told them they couldn't do anything and they'd have to take the matter up with the senior officers. What happened was, they got everybody out of that camp – in 24 hours the men were all lining up, getting into trains and off! They cleared the lot out.

Sergeant Guy Buckeridge
Royal Engineers

There was a riot in our Division here. The fellows declined to march and carry full packs. The war was over for them, and they refused to be pack animals any longer. It all seemed very foolish to me, but the authorities very wisely conceded what was asked for and in the end our spare gear was carried for us.

On 13th December my leave warrant was handed to me. The next day found me at Bavay, where I stayed in charge of a billet until the 17th. The weather was awful and the men fractious. Rations were bad. They hated being delayed in reaching their homes and the transport commandant had a difficult and thankless task. There were several riots and he eventually appealed to all NCOs to help to make things work. But it was hopeless. The continual rain and lack of amusement gave the fellows no chance of getting outside to air their immediate grievances.

The 18th found me at Cambrai, where we were put in the barracks. The feeling was no better there and I was glad to leave. It seemed as though the whole Army had become imbued with a spirit of revolt against the system which had held the individual for so long.

Major Alfred Bundy
In Salonika
(in his diary)
November 17

Yesterday we had the first arrival of about 600 men, and they are difficult to handle. Hundreds of men have arrived daily. Strangely enough, now that the war is over, numbers of the men refuse to obey orders – or rather, they show a degree of independence that is most disconcerting. I had to talk to a whole company that were disgracefully abusive to their officers. I realized that any show of military authority would be fatal, so I reasoned with them and told them that for the benefit of all, and in order to facilitate the movement of those who were anxious to get back to England, it was necessary that they should still behave as disciplined soldiers. My remarks were greeted by cat-calls and rude noises, but I knew that there must be a large proportion of the men who were anxious to assist me in the performance of my duty and in facilitating their return to England, so I announced that if there was obstruction, I should have the offenders arrested and kept back. There was then almost complete silence, and I had no further difficulty.

Over the period until 6 February, it seems there's been nothing exciting except reports of murder, robbery and rioting. If this is peace, war is better!

Corporal Edgar Woolley
14 Squadron, Royal Flying Corps

We were pleased to be home in England and we were looking forward to the sort of welcome that we'd heard of in the song, that said we should be welcomed and kissed on our arrival, but in fact the atmosphere and reception which greeted us was more like one for returned jail escapers.

We were directed to a hut with a concrete floor, given a couple of blankets, and told to make ourselves as comfortable as we could. None of us had had any money for many weeks. We were hoping to get a decent meal, and they had nothing to offer us, and the men were getting very disappointed with the reception and conditions – and they wanted to know what was going to be done about it. They started marching round the camp, singing out 'We want food', 'We want money', trying to make some protest against their treatment.

The following day, the Camp Commander called us all together in the hut. He addressed us, 'Look here you men. We don't want any trouble here – and if we have any trouble, I've got some machine guns here.' One of our men had been in the infantry in Gallipoli and Egypt and he immediately jumped up and said, 'We've faced machine guns before, sir, and we can face them again. Who are you going to get to use them, anyway?' Apparently this very much impressed the CO – it was a spirit that appealed to him. He asked, 'What is your trouble?' So one or two voices struck up – 'We've got no money, we haven't had a decent meal, we can't supplement the horrid food we're getting with anything bought from outside – and what we want is something on account of the money owing to us.'

The CO asked one of them, 'What do you want?' He said, 'I want £10, sir.' So the CO said, 'You can have it. Now, I'm going to arrange for you chaps to have some money.' Later he said to me, 'what do you want, Corporal?' I said, 'I could do with £10 as well, sir.' He said, 'All right – you'll have it.' True to his word, the following day he got us some money to build up our wasted resources.

Private Leonard Davies
Royal Air Force

After the Armistice we were ordered to fly over to Germany and occupy an aerodrome. We were one of the first squadrons to do this. We landed at the aerodrome, where the Germans' Zeppelin was housed.

We were there for at least a week, and then we flew back to France. When we got back, it was a question then of when we would be disbanded. I asked our CO how long that was going to take, and he said, 'Oh, months I expect.' This made me wonder why I should wait about for months – after all, the war was over.

I knew that in war, if anybody disobeyed orders, showed any signs of cowardice or tried running off, that the penalty would be extremely high – and I felt that the same sort of thing must still apply now, otherwise if everybody started to do what I did, there would be panic all over the shop, and you wouldn't get on the boats. All the same, I thought that I would try – but I didn't ask any pals to try it with me – I just went off on my own.

I packed a few things in a haversack and made my way to Boulogne. There was a troop ship waiting there, and I simply got into one of the queues which were boarding it, and I don't think I was recognized, but a corporal said to me, 'Where are you from?' So I said I was from the army. He said, 'Which regiment?' I said I didn't know and I argued with him for a bit and in the end I think I gave him a 5-Franc note and he just said 'Ok, get on'. There were an awful lot of other people, all strangers to me – and a lot were strangers to each other too. I had one or two things in my haversack that I'd carried all the way through the war including a German helmet. We were lined up on the side of the ship and an officer came along to inspect us, I felt sure that if he saw the helmet I would be sent off, so I tipped it overboard. But I did have in my bag a German magneto, because I thought I could have a bit of fun with that when I got home.

We landed at Dover and were disembarked – and when we had to show our papers the official didn't even read my form, so I got back without a problem. I phoned up my brother who was in the Air Force. He came to meet me and I was awfully pleased to see him. We were both in Air Force uniform, but he was now an officer, while I still spoke like a trooper. While I was talking to him, a military policeman came up and said, 'I am afraid that I have got to arrest you.' I asked what for, and he said, 'Because you have deserted the Army.' I said I didn't think I had – in fact I had joined the war for the duration and the war was over – so I'd just come home. All the same, he said, 'I'm afraid you'll have to come up with something better than that.' Anyway, my brother took the case up and got in touch with somebody in the Air Force, who was able to say that it was perfectly all right – that I was justified in doing what I did as far as the Air Force was concerned, and they wouldn't take it any further.

Private William Easton
77th Field Ambulances, RAMC

We prisoners got out of Holland, but I never was demobbed. I just had fifteen days' leave. We came back to England and the insult of it we were put into a camp and weren't allowed out – barbed wire all round. In the next camp there were captured German sailors – but they were allowed out on parole while we had to stay in. Some of our chaps kicked up the devil of a row – they said they'd break out and they wouldn't wait on any army law, so in the end they let us out. Ripon was about four miles away, and they told us to go there. Some of us were half dead when we got there, and we found there were no shops open, no lights, and everywhere cold as ice. We walked back and we found all these women, waiting to go out with these blinking German soldiers or sailors. There looked like being quite a riot.

Next morning the eight o'clock bugle was blown – but the men didn't take any notice, and they didn't get up. We were in our huts, frozen to the marrow. The sergeant came in and said, 'You are still under army law – so you will get up. Otherwise you will be put in the enclosure on your own.' If he'd tried it, there would have been blue murder. There was a proper revolt. Nobody would get up, so along came a poor scrap of an old colonel. 'What's the matter with you lads?' and somebody said, 'What would you say if you weren't allowed out while the Germans were out with all the women?' He said that shouldn't have happened, and he told his sergeant off. Then, when they ordered us to fall in – get up and get out – nobody shifted. There were about fifty of us and we just sat there. In the end we did get up and they promised us they would get us away from there, just as soon as they got the order.

But this wasn't good enough and there was a lot of argument about it. It looked like the chaps were up for a break out – most of them had been POWs and they didn't think much of these prison conditions back at home. Eventually they took down our particulars, and it must have been something special, because at dinner time we each got vouchers to go home. I had to get to York, then down to Peterborough. It was awful. I never got anything to eat, so I was famished. I ended up on March station in the middle of the night, and caught the last train to Lymne. We got in in the early morning and I went home.

I felt very rough about how the army treated me. Not least, was the fact that they knew half the time I was in the army I was ill, but I never got any treatment. When I came back I was put on night duty, of all things, Southmead Hospital outside Bristol – that was the best hospital the army had. In the war the army took it over, but they had to give it up. Even so, I finally got a staff job, and they kept me there two years. First of all I was a nursing orderly, and I had forty limbless men to look after on my night shift. Eventually I got out of it and was demobbed.

Corporal Tommy Keele
11th Battalion Middlesex Regiment; attached to 'Ace of Spades'
Concert Party

I wondered when I'd get demobbed – this seemed to be happening in dribs and drabs. One day somebody would get a letter that they were up for demobilization, and the next day they would be sent to Boulogne, then on to England. Gradually everyone drifted away. The last two left were me and Bert Waterworth, my pal.

The first thing we wanted was to get back to England. I was looking forward to it, but it wasn't to be a happy homecoming. My father died in 1918, but they wouldn't give me compassionate leave to come back for his funeral. One sister had gone to America, and my eldest sister sold up the hotel my father had owned in King's Cross. She practically gave it away, so on returning to London I had no home, nowhere to go and no family left. Even so, I was still looking forward to civilian life.

I think the country was keen to get as many people demobbed and back into civil life as they could. Bert and I were the last two from the band, so we were left with all this gear from the concert parties. The army didn't seem to want it, so we said, 'Let's have a jumble sale'. So we circulated around the village, asking, 'Do you want to buy a nice dress suit?' or, 'Would you like some costumes – or curtains?' We had quite a jumble sale and we sold nearly everything.

I had been in the concert party about eighteen months, and we lived a decent life. We kept clean – you could have baths and we had a lot of our own underwear. But when we got to Boulogne the army said that everybody had to be de-loused and go for physical examination to see if we had any diseases. I tried to tell them I was clean, but like everyone else, I paraded in front of the medical officer, stripped to just my boots on and cap. This geezer had a small-toothed comb which he ran through your hair and under your armpits and round by your private parts. We were clean – I hadn't got anything there – but believe you me, in a couple of days' time my private parts were absolutely lousy. This geezer must have had some old nits left in his comb, they had taken root in my hair and I was as lousy as I'd been during my years in the trenches.

In Boulogne we handed in our rifles and ammunition, then we were shipped back to England. We were sent to Crystal Palace, where we were kitted out with civilian suits, shoes and hats – and that was the end. I saw so many officers – you'd see a full colonel walking in one door and coming out half an hour later in this funny civilian suit.

I had no job or family, so I had nowhere to go. I gave myself a month. I'd stay in England a month, and if I hadn't sorted myself out within that month I would apply to emigrate to America and join my sister in New York. But on the last day of that month I landed a job in a concert party going to Sidmouth, and that started me on my theatrical career.

Lance Corporal A J Abraham

Back in England, I was sent to Connaught Military Hospital, Aldershot, which was very different from the draughty huts we had become accustomed to in France. Although it looked like a workhouse, it was solid, clean and warm – beds with sheets and plenty of blankets – and by now we were not lousy. We were in paradise.

On 30 January 1919 I had my final medical board and was asked to sign a declaration that I was leaving the army in a perfect state of health. I was not, but at that time I think I would have signed a declaration saying I was Lloyd George if that was what it took to get my release – so I put my signature to the document without a qualm.

A group of us walked to Aldershot Station, took the train to London, and at Victoria we parted and went our separate ways to start living again. Like every demobilized soldier at that time, I had a month's leave on full pay, then handed in my great-coat at the nearest railway station, receiving £1 in exchange. As soon as my civilian suit was ready for me I discarded my uniform, although I had to keep it, as I was on the 'Z' Reserve for many years.

Sergeant B W Carmichael

I had been wounded in the last week of the war, and I found myself in a convalescent camp in bell tents. I was sharing with two other sergeants and a sergeant major from a Scottish regiment. I heard somebody outside the tent ask if there was a Sergeant Carmichael there – and I stood at the door of the tent and said, 'Yes! Me!' It was my brother, Joe, who was a Sergeant in the King's Own Scottish Borderers, who with his pal had borrowed army bikes and ridden over from Le Treport.

We'd not met each other since early 1915, and he remarked to his mate that I'd been a school kid then. My father had been very worried when he'd been informed I'd been injured, and had managed to get a message to him to get over to see me.

I took them up to what we described as the Sergeants' Mess for tea. On the tables were loaves of bread, half cartons of jam and butter with enamel mugs of tea, good condensed-milky tea, a rare sight then to me, and I told them to help themselves as though they were at a party. They had both been through the mill, but were absolutely disgusted that this was the way we were being treated, and more shocked still that I had reached the state where I could accept this as the sort of convalescent food and housing fit for NCOs who had been through it and now needed some comfort.

Anything at that time, by comparison, was good to me, but I quickly realized how we had been used as rubbish and there was little doubt that a great deal of our shortages, and yes, suffering, for such it was, was due to sheer damn bad organization – at more than battalion level and in the matter of food and supplies we maybe got about a quarter of what was due to us.

As an instance of this, and months later when I was back with the battalion as CQM Sergeant and checking equipment, in the Regimental QM stores I found leather and canvas bags with pockets, very much like golf bags. I challenged the then RQM

Sergeant, 'How long have you had these?' as I had never heard of or seen such things. When he told me they had been carting them to and fro for months, I was speechless. There we had been, in and out of the line with Lewis guns plastered with clay and mud, full of rainwater, so that the gun wouldn't fire – and here were Lewis gun covers in store, unissued so that the books could be kept straight. From a disciplined soldier, as I had always considered myself to be, I'm afraid that I now turned more than a bit rebellious. I had soon got fed up with hospital and convalescent camp. The Armistice had been signed – although I personally did not see or take part in any celebrations. I had got myself discharged sooner than was wise, as my legs were still giving me trouble. Months after I returned home, my brother thought I was mad not to see the doctor and have them attended to, as they were still not healed, but I'd had enough.

Private Raynor Taylor
Welch Regiment

When I eventually got demobbed I got a suit – it was thick, and had no blooming style about it – jackets were just straight. I don't think we got a cap, but you could retain your army overcoat – because they didn't give you a coat. If, after you had been demobilized, you took your coat to a railway station they'd give you £1 for it. For a long time after the war there were military great coats in use because people hadn't handed them in. Despite what anybody said, it was jolly good, hard wearing stuff.

When you were demobilized there was no way you could check up what pay was owed to you – you just accepted what they said was credited to you. Just before I was demobbed I had to go before a pensions board, because I'd lost a finger. Everyone who'd been injured had to do that. They examined me, and saw the stump – but these army officers had no idea that this finger was so important to me for my work. The man that examined me wasn't sympathetic at all, and eventually I was awarded just 12.5% disability pension – which I never drew because they wrote to me later to say that this pension had been commuted into £30 as a final payment – and that was the end of it.

It was some time in 1919, and we three brothers were all home together – and it was the first time we were all in uniform. I think we were on demobilization leave. My father said, 'I want you to go and have your photo taken, all together in uniform.' There was a photographer just over the road and we had a photo taken – that was the only time we were all together – then our father bought us a celebration drink.

He asked us to join him at the Hollinwood Institute. They had a reading room there in those days with newspapers and glossy magazines, where members could go and relax. That was where he would spend his free afternoons, reading *The Tatler*, *The Illustrated London News* and *Punch* and the morning papers. As we went in, I could see my dad get up from where he sat reading, 'Ee, hello,' he said, 'come on in.' He took us to the bar, where there were quite a few other members. 'These are my lads!' he said. They probably knew that, but they'd never seen us all together before. He went up to the bar and said to our Albert, 'What will thou have Albert?' 'Oh I'll have a pint.' And that spoiled my dad's day – ruined it. Our Albert had left home a seventeen-year-old boy, who went to Sunday school three times a Sunday – and the next time he comes into contact with his father, he is ordering a pint of beer! He only ordered him a half. Then he said to my other brother, 'What will thou have?' 'I won't say no to a pint,' he was the eldest. He then looked at me, and before I had a chance to say anything he said that I'd have a shandy – and that's what I got. We were three returning servicemen, and we got a pint and a half of beer and a shandy – that was our reward. He never got used to the fact that we had grown up.

The Colonel and men of the 9th East Surreys celebrating the news of the
Armistice at St Waast, near Laval in France.

Armistice Day outside Buckingham Palace.

19th July 1919. The victory march in London with British troops passing out of Whitehall into Trafalgar Square.

Women at the Royal Army Clothing Department, Battersea Park, London, preparing to dispatch thousands of demob suits.

Ten months after the war a group of unemployed ex-servicemen carry a banner demanding work, during the Great Railway Strike.

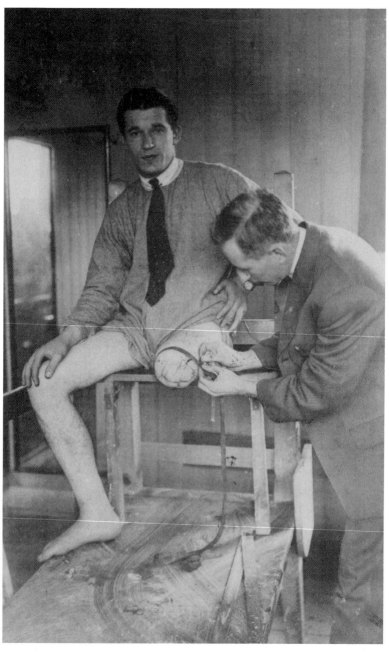

At Roehampton Hospital an amputee is being measured for a new leg.

At Roehampton Hospital patients being taught to use their new artificial limbs.

Disabled veterans learn a new craft at a factory on the Old Kent Road, London: Mr F. Jackson, who lost an arm, and Mr H. Grinter, DCM MM, who lost both legs in the war, manufacture cornflowers for the Ypres League.

The skeletons of the New Zealand forces left unburied at Anzac Cove, Gallipoli.

Removing remains
from wet ground.
A deeply moving task
particularly if they
were known to you.

The remains awaiting
removal to a cemetery.

Tyne Cot cemetery seen here in 1919, is the largest British war cemetery in the world. 11,908 graves are registered within Tyne Cot. Of this total 70% are unknown. Today on the wall at the back of the cemetery are the names of 34,927 soldiers who have no known grave and died from August 1917 to the end of the war.

King George V presenting widows with their husbands' medals at Buckingham Palace.

1920 British Legion pilgrimage to Vimy Ridge. Mothers and widows are buying wreaths for their son's or husband's grave at the cemetery.

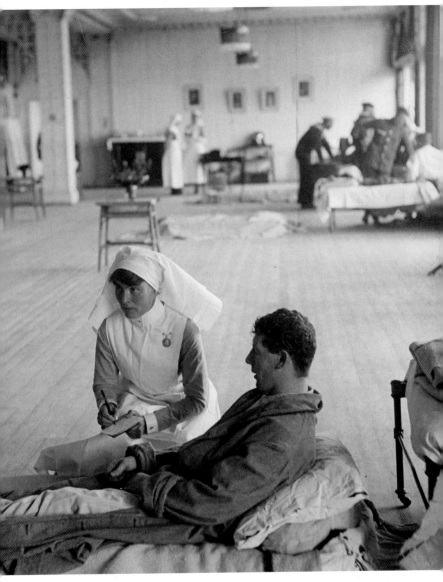

May 1919: Sister Maycock writing her address for a patient at Queen Mary's Hospital in Southend, just before it closed down.

January 1919: Mutinous soldiers demonstrating peacefully against being sent to Russia. There were further mutinies by British troops in Russia.

A year after the end of the war: a destitute family in Fleet Street, London.

The body of the Unknown Warrior has been selected and, with dignity, is beginning his last journey.

November 1920: The coffin of the Unknown Warrior is carried from the Citadel in Boulogne, on its way to his final resting place in Westminster Abbey.

11 November 1920: The unveiling of the Cenotaph by King George V in Whitehall. On the same day the Unknown Warrior was buried.

Private Walter Hare

15th Battalion West Yorkshire Regiment

The first day home, at dinner time, there was just my mother, father and me at home, but there were seven places laid at the table. I asked why, when there were only three of us. My mother said, 'We have some German prisoners working in the brick works and I try to make them a bit of dinner, because I thought the Germans would be looking after you.' I said, 'Mother, they gave us nothing. I went down to seven stone.' 'Yes – but you are back home and they're still here.' She was that sort of woman. 'I thought I would make them a bit of dinner – and I thought you could take it out to them.' I said, 'All right, mother – put a bit of arsenic on it and I will take it out.' She said, 'Don't be like that – at least you are back home.' So I said I'd take the food out to the German prisoners – a plateful of the same food as we were having. I told her about the conditions in Germany but she wouldn't believe me. There was one Bavarian chap there – he was nice and he wanted to have a talk about what they had done to us.

It was just a day later that my brother got home – and my mother was so relieved. She kept saying, 'He's not coming back. I know it. I know it. You might as well tell me the truth.' I said, 'No you WILL finally see him tomorrow.' And she did.

We got a fortnight's leave, and I began to eat normally again – but I had to be careful. We had been warned that after being starved for so long, we could do ourselves more harm than good. The day after my leave ended, I had to report to York, and the day after that I went up to Whitley Bay to a convalescent home. We were treated very well there, and we didn't do any parades or work. We were there as invalids, to get ourselves better again.

I couldn't wait to be demobilized. I wanted to get out as quickly as I could. I'd had more than enough of the army. I'd joined up for the duration and the duration had come and gone. Now I wanted to be back in civilian life. We got forms to fill and

I realized that it depended very much on what sort of work you did, how and when you were demobilized. There were certain areas of industry where they wanted to get you back at work. Unfortunately mine wasn't very important. My father ran brick-works, and I knew bricks would be required because there was a lot of building and repair work to be done. I said to my father, 'If I put myself down as a brick and tile worker, can you find me a job for a week or two?' He said he could, so I put that on the form and I got an early discharge.

The only thing I do resent is to do with my health. I went in as A1, and I came out B2. At the only examination I got after the war, they checked my heart and took my pulse – saw I was still breathing and said I was A1 – but I should have been classed as B2. I ought to have pressed them about that, because I had been gassed and slightly wounded and been reduced to a terrible state. I ought to have pressed for another examination, but I just wanted to be out. One friend of mine got a wound in his eye the first day in action. He got a full pension for the rest of his life. That is what I objected to! One day in the trenches, he got a small wound and was awarded a full pension. I got nothing.

If you had a job before the war and you volunteered to join up, they had to give you your job back after the war. When I went back to my old job, the boss had got a couple of girls in. We had a chat and the manager said that the girls would have to leave because I wanted my job back, but he said that he would rather keep them on. I said we'd see about that, but then one day my mother told me that a man who owned two shops in the village – a grocers and a chemist – would like to see me. He asked me if I'd like to work for him, and I said I'd love to. He said he'd pay me £2 10 shillings a week – and I didn't know what money was worth, but it was more than I had been getting when I joined up.

Corporal Hawtin Mundy
5th Battalion, Oxfordshire and Buckinghamshire Light Infantry

When I eventually got home, I knocked on the back door and I heard my mother come down – then my dad, with my little brother – and we had a nice reunion. My mother got out a bottle of whisky – she said she had got it a long time ago, specially for when I came home. We sat chatting for a long time, then eventually my mother broke down and began praying and giving thanks to God for bringing me home safely. How lovely it was to be back at home after all those hardships!

In the morning I wandered around the house, having a look around. I got out the breakfast things and got the sausages on, then my mother came down. 'You go back to bed – I'll cook for you.' Then she said, 'I don't know how you are going to eat those! That's the pan with the fish fat.'

A few days later I had notification from the record office and my pay started to come through, then £20 demob and two years' back pay. It all came to about £100. I thought, 'Oh! I'm a millionaire.' I'd got three months' leave, and I thought that money would last me a lifetime. But oh no – it went all right. As soon as the three months was up, I had to start work again.

I was paired up all right, so before I started back to work, I said to my girl, 'Before I go back to work, I think we ought to see if I can afford for us to get wed.' So we both put our names down together and carried on. We carried on for 54 years! I picked a diamond, and my god, how that diamond sparkled for 54 years.

CHAPTER 5

Lives Changed For Ever

Badly injured and permanently disabled men were repatriated for treatment and to convalesce throughout the war, but with the end of hostilities, the authorities and medical institutions turned their attention to the plight of amputees, the seriously scarred and disfigured, and the disabled.

Doctors and specialist manufacturers collaborated to design and test false limbs – which were now in massive demand. For those who had returned with facial injuries, far from sharing the joyous welcome which awaited their unscathed comrades, they were a living reminder of the horrors of battle – as they were often too terrifying to look at. Every effort had to be made to make their appearance more palatable and give them some hope of acceptance in society.

For all these men there were issues of grants and disability pensions to consider – but some bore invisible scars. Many men, shattered by shellshock, still suffered the haunting terror of their experiences – and not all got the sympathy their condition deserved. Too traumatized to rejoin society, many were taken into hospitals run by the Lunacy Board of Control to be 'snapped out of it'. A minority – the officers – were accorded more enlightened treatment in small, specialized clinics, but neurasthenia, or post-traumatic stress, was a condition the military found hard to deal with.

Other men and women whose political persuasions and consciences dictated that they reject the war from the start, and would not allow them to fight, found themselves still reviled, even after serving their time in prison. They too were victims of the war, and they walked free to face a future achieved through the sacrifice of others – their lives would not be easy.

Private Joseph Pickard

Northumberland Fusiliers

I was hit underneath the joint of the leg, and the shrapnel had sliced through the sciatic nerve, chipping both hip joints. It also smashed the left side of my pelvis and made three holes in the bladder, and I lost my nose. What a bloody mess! Oh dear! I crawled along the road on my hands and knees, and I saw a fellow I knew and I shouted out to him and somebody got a stretcher and there was a Red Cross van pulled up near the bottom of the road. They carried me through the barrage and I got into the wagon. One fellow said, 'You'll be alright now chum.'

I lost consciousness, then I remember coming round in this advance clearing station and it was dark. I was lying on a stretcher and I didn't know what was the matter with me. It turned out there was a blanket over the top of me, and I'd been left for dead. The old lady back home got the number of my grave, and the King and Queen's sympathy.

When my parents first got the news that I'd been killed, my mother didn't believe it. Maybe it was second sight or intuition, but my father later told me that she was baking bread when the telegram came. She just set it aside, then someone asked her about it – and she simply said, 'No – it's not true.'

I was sent to the Ford Western General Hospital in Neath, in Glamorgan and I was there from May until January 1919. It was a matter of waiting until all the bones knitted together in the left side of the pelvis. The doctor worked on and on, and I was up and down to the operating theatre until he was satisfied.

With my nose, they just kept the blinking bandages across it, and I had to eat and shave around it. I got fed up with this and one day I said to the sister, 'Give us a loan of your scissors'. I cut all these blinking bandages off to have a look at it – and my nose had gone, half way across the bridge.

She asked me if it bothered me – and to be honest, I didn't feel it did. She was a bit dubious and said, 'What do you think about it?' I said, 'What can I do? It's gone, I don't think I will be travelling along the trench line to look for it.' She said she felt it would get better. I never let myself get depressed about it. At one time I was knocking about London with no nose – and no teeth!

Can you ever imagine being without a nose? I never put the bandages back on. I got a piece of plastic to put across the hole where my nose had been. But there was only one occasion when I felt badly about my nose – or lack of it. I was in Neath and it was the first time I went out of the hospital – I wanted to have a look around the town. All the houses were built on a hillside in rows, and I was going along the bottom of the valley where there were some kids playing. A while after I passed, they suddenly galloped up past me. I went on past two or three streets and when I got to the end, all the kids in the neighbourhood had gathered. They were all talking, looking, gawping at me. I could have taken my crutch and hit the whole blinking lot of them. I knew what they were looking at, so I turned around and went straight back to hospital. I was sitting there later and I thought, 'Well, I could be stuck like this for the rest of my life. No use sitting moping. You've got to face it sometime.' So I went out again, and after that anytime I went anywhere I just walked out without thinking about it.

No-one made fun of me before I had the new nose – although people did stare. I never understood why they did that. I used to turn around and look back at them.

I got back to Newcastle, to what was Armstrong College which is now King's College. I had to start treatment all over again with my leg. The shrapnel had severed my sciatic nerve – and I've still got a dead foot, and always have to wear boots rather than shoes. I had to attend an orthopaedic board – where they discussed my case. They said they would operate on my nose and they also opened up my hip and found the two ends of the sciatic nerve then sewed them together.

Not long after that, I was able to walk along by the side of the bed, with one foot on the floor. I had an enormous boot with two straps – they called it an 'elephant's foot' – but I was able to walk with a stick. I was there until July 1919. When I first went to Newcastle, after the board consultation, I made it quite clear that no matter whatever happened I wanted to be sent to St Mary's at Sidcup.

They had a plastic surgery clinic there for face cases – and I was to have a new nose put on. I was there about two years in total, being treated by Professor Kilner. First of all they took photographs, then I went to a small hut where my face was smothered with plaster of Paris. They made a mask, and when it hardened and was taken off, it showed up every little blemish on the face. Gradually, after various operations, such as a rib graft, they reopened my nostrils and cleaned the area up.

As part of my plastic surgery, they cut down the right side of my ribs and took out a lot of cartilage. Then they cut down to the left side of the stomach and grafted it in there, keeping it alive. Then when they were ready, they cut a piece off and grafted it on to the bridge of my nose to build it up. The first graft went wrong. The doctor asked me, 'What have you been doing? It shouldn't have gone like that.' I replied, 'Well, you grafted it.' You could really talk to the doctors, and they and the nurses would do anything for you.

There was some event happening one day and Kilner was in the ward. He had seen various fellows and they all wanted to go to a dance. I went in to see him with my papers – I ended up with a file several inches thick – and as I went in he said, 'I suppose you want to go dancing?' 'Aye if I could have a couple of new legs,' I replied. Then we got on to my nose – and he didn't see anybody else after that. With all these men wanting to go to this dance, it meant if I went in the operating theatre he'd have all day to work on it. So he went to the office and got my mask, and asked me, 'What do you want – a Wellington nose or a Roman nose?' I said I didn't care what, as long as I got one. He started to run through exactly what he was going to do, and I told the sister that I'd have my operation in the morning.

I went in at nine o'clock the next morning and the next thing I knew it was the middle of the next night. A little while later, this pal came by and said, 'My God, what a lovely little nose you've got!' I couldn't raise me head off the pillow – I had two black eyes and a square chin – so he went away and fetched a mirror and showed me myself with the magnifying side. The blinking nose seemed to fill the whole mirror!

I was quite happy with my new nose. I didn't care what it was like, just as long as I'd got one. Life wasn't the same without one. Later on I went up to Roehampton, which is a big hospital – a wonderful place with a lot of underground operating theatres and excellent facilities. The last time I was there, Kilner came in while I was in the waiting room. As he came up the corridor he was asking, 'Where's Pickard? Come here.' He had all his students with him and we were sitting round a table with a nursing sister in attendance. Suddenly he asked, 'Where's the bit of extra stuff you've got?' 'Oh it's still here,' said the sister – it was a piece of my cartilage, just in case anything got knocked out or broken. When I was only about nine stone, my new cartilage nose used to stand out like a piece of marble!

I never walked properly again, and never really regained my sense of smell, and one nostril is pretty well closed. I had a pair of silver 'nostrils' that I wore for a long time to keep the passages open, but I got careless. I kept them out for so long I couldn't get them back in place. I thought if I get another two of them I could make them into a pair of cufflinks.

Gunner William Towers
Royal Field Artillery

I got involved working with BLESMA – the British Limbless Ex-Servicemen's Association.

We got to know all limbless men and where they lived – and somehow we circulated the news among them when there was any sort of gathering. One day we heard there was going to be a meeting at the town hall where they were enrolling people in an association, and we went along.

There were several ex-officers at the meeting who were now accountants, solicitors and barristers – all big people and like everyone there they were missing a limb – a leg, an arm or an eye. A fellow called Cyril Stevens stood up and started the meeting. 'First of all, gentlemen, welcome. The first thing you need to do is propose somebody as chairman.' We were having a lot of trouble with the people who fitted the limbs in those days – this was in 1930 – they were fitting us with cheap legs and getting away with it. Some bright spark proposed a Mr Holden and someone seconded that. But this was the funny part – Mr Holden was a fitter of cheap legs in Chapel Allerton. He then asked if we would propose a secretary – and someone proposed Holden's yes-man. It was as stupid as a big factory forming a union and putting the manager in as chairman of the union. I said it was one of the most ridiculous things I'd ever heard. I left and I didn't go back for a long time.

It was a real problem – there was a company called Deseutre making a really beautiful leg – but these people were fitting a cheap version. How often you'd need to replace your leg would vary. Generally this would need to be done every five or six years. If you wanted a repair, and they considered it would cost over a certain percentage of the total cost, they'd scrap the old leg.

On one occasion I went for a repair – but the doctor said he thought it was better to scrap the leg altogether and get a new one. I went to get this new leg measured – the doctor had given me a chit to present at the fitting centre. When I arrived, there was Holden and I said, 'I don't want one of your legs.' He said, 'You'll bloody well have to have one – or do without.' I asked why, and he said 'Because you can't have anything else.' So he made me a leg – and it never fitted me. I told him this, and he said it was just me being awkward.

The new leg wasn't the right shape for me. They made fitted legs to a standard shape – but not all men match the standard. This leg was nipping my flesh all the time as I walked and it caused abscesses. Eventually I had to go into hospital and have surgery to remove them. All five wards of the hospital were full and quite a few of the patients had the same trouble as me.

All of a sudden they started bringing bed patients items such as brass ashtrays to polish, and if you were up and walking about you had to clean the radiator taps. We were expecting royalty at least. However, when the door opened, a man came in whom we didn't recognize, followed by two or three others. He went to the first bed and said, 'Now, young man, how are you?' 'Very well sir.' They had a chat and then he went to the next bed. 'How are you?' 'Very well, sir.' The chap next to me said, 'What a lot of hypocrites! Of course they're all very well. They're in bed.'

This new chap came to me – and I didn't know then that he was a doctor. I'd been in there for months, and my blood was boiling. I was getting really worked up. He got to me and asked, 'And how are you?' I said, 'I am NOT very well sir.' He peered at me and said, 'Why is that?' I said, 'I wouldn't be in this bed if I was very well. I would be working. I do have a job.' He asked me what my problem was, and I told him I had abscesses on my stump. 'How did you get them?' I told him that it was from wearing a cheap, inferior leg. When he asked me who made it, I explained that it was so cheap, they didn't put their name on it – they just stamped AL Ltd on it.'

He had a whispered conversation with one of the surgeons,

then I said, 'Don't take my word for it. You have my papers here – I was discharged in 1918 and it's now 1936. I have never needed any treatment in all that time – until my leg was fitted on the cheap. Not only that – seventy per cent of them in here are in the same boat, suffering from wearing a cheap leg. It's costing you ten times more than if you paid for us to have decent legs.'

This man Holden was part of a consortium of firms who got together to make these cheap legs under contract, and the old companies making quality legs had been scrapped. Nowadays there's a Swedish firm making a new, ultra modern leg, thirty-five per cent cheaper than those old legs – it's a much better leg and they fit them a different way, but I am an old man now. My old doctor always said, 'Never have a leg altered Bill, keep it as it is.' We found out that this outfit were altering people's legs so that they could no longer wear them, so they'd have to go to the doctor. The doc would condemn the leg and they would have to buy a new one. I ended up with this one – and I can walk about, but not as well as I used to. I never walked with a stick until I had this last leg altered.

I felt that the worst thing was that nobody ever explained to me how things could be arranged and what was going to happen to me. I always used to dress very smartly – I had a job and I could walk well, so I decided I'd go to the local hospital and talk with new amputees – show how much you can do with a false leg. I met up with people from BLESMA there, and I joined up to work with them. They used to look forward to my visits.

Among the fellows I met there was one who had a wounded leg and could hardly walk. He was in agony all the time and couldn't really walk and he had to put his leg upon a box at work and take tablets to kill the pain. I thought about it, and said, 'Actually I wouldn't stick it if I were you. I would have it taken off.' I suggested that he have his leg amputated so that he would be free of all the pain, and be able to walk about. He thought

about it and said, 'If I can walk like you, I'll let them take it off.'
He had it amputated and he never looked back.

Private Harry Davies
8th Battalion, Black Watch

I'd got a shrapnel ball in my left knee – but there wasn't a spoonful
of blood when I was wounded, and there was very little pain.

All our transport had disappeared – even the Red Cross vans.
Eventually I got away with an artillery lorry to a little field station
where I got a dressing, then I walked as far to the rear as I could.
After going a quarter of a mile, I thought they'd put the bandage
on very tight, and I eased it off. In a couple of hours my leg had
swollen up enormously.

It was four days before I got any proper dressing for my leg –
by which time gangrene had set in. I reached a real field station
where they operated and took the bullet out. I thought this wasn't
enough to get me out of the war – but it turned to gangrene and
they told me they wanted my permission to do whatever they felt
it needed. I said, 'Do anything – but you don't want to take my
leg off, do you?' They said that it might well come to that, so
they needed my permission. I said to go ahead – they knew better
than I did. I never dreamed of losing a leg.

At first they cut a big slit along the front and along the side of
my leg to let the bad blood out, and I thought that would cure it.
I didn't even think it would be enough to keep me away from the
war – but it proved otherwise. I had the operation to remove the
leg, then after about ten days I came back to England.

Beechbury Park was a home from home except that it had
doctors and nurses. I was there for five months with a running
wound. When I first had my leg off, they stitched it up beautifully.
I got a mirror the next day to examine it, and they had made a
wonderful job of it. Four nights later they came and took my

temperature and pulse. I heard the doctor tell the nurse to 'open it up'. They had to burst the stitches open – and that was painful. I then had a running wound in my leg, which later proved to be caused by a piece of shrapnel that had been left in when they'd first sewn it up. I went from a healthy lad to a shadow and I lost my hair. The first time I was fitted with an artificial leg I was at Roehampton for six weeks until they'd made the leg, then I had a week to practise walking on it. When I first got it, I thought, 'If I walk a hundred yards with this I'll deserve a Victoria Cross.' But I went home a week later, and the next day I went for a cycle ride – but I was only a lad then.

It was thirty-eight years before I had the stump resewn, but I have a wonderful stump now. I know how long it was because I was attending a limb-fitting hospital in Leeds. The surgeon never saw your leg – he saw you with a wooden or a metal leg on, and if you walked all right, he'd not bother to examine your stump. I was due for an examination – something to do with pensions, because I had been wrongly assessed. The doctor was just about to feel my stump and I said, 'For goodness sake don't touch it. I'll jump a mile!' If I touched it myself, or if Mrs Davies' nightdress touched it, I would nearly leap out of bed, it was so sensitive. The surgeon asked how long it had been like that, and I told him, 'Thirty-eight years'. I got a ten per cent increase in my pension after that examination.

I used to play golf, I drove a car – an ordinary one without any special fittings. Even though I have only a very short stump, I used my artificial leg for the clutch. I lost my wife after fifty-eight years and I remarried the most wonderful woman in the world – an absolute marvel. She encouraged me to go to Leeds and ask to try one of these new suction-end legs. I saw a doctor and he was a treasure – he said, 'Try it by all means – it's wonderful at nearly ninety to want to try something new.'

I got this new leg – it was all pink plastic and padding. I found it bulky and I couldn't sit with my legs crossed – and I'd thought it would be a lot lighter, but it wasn't due to all the padding. So I went back to the old one. It's never got me down, my leg. I have never felt sorry for myself. I always thought about what I'd got, not what I had lost. I still think the same way. I've been blind for fifteen years, but I don't think I've ever complained once. I lost my hearing, which was absolutely acute, and I still have a shocking cough from the gas.

They never gave me any allowance for the effects of the gas. If I'd had four toes off I would have got four shillings a week less in pension than I did for losing my leg.

There isn't a happier man in the world than me today – and there isn't a happier woman than my wife. She lost her husband about ten years ago, and they'd been friends of ours before my first wife died. It isn't much good being on your own when you can't see, and I had to go to a home for limbless ex-servicemen. All the same, I rang her up every day for about five years, and she said it helped her keep her reason after she lost her husband. We were always great friends before, and I never stopped ringing her each morning. She's told me since we got married that she used to look forward to this. She used to come and get meals ready for me, and I got very fond of her. I said to her that if I was fifteen years younger, I'd ask her to marry me. She said, that the way she felt about me, if I needed nursing, she'd want to nurse me – so we got married, and it's the most wonderful thing that has ever happened.

Lieutenant Jim Davies
9th Battalion, Royal Fusiliers

I was wounded in the leg by machine-gun fire in no-man's-land, then after getting shrapnel wounds in my knee, I had my leg amputated at the casualty clearing station.

When I got back to England in 1918, I was sent to the hospital in Somerville College, Oxford. It was very nice there. When I first went there, I used to lie out in a bed under a tree, watching all the wounded being brought in from the RAF – those poor boys learning to be airmen didn't last very long.

The other problem was that there was a wound right through my remaining leg – a great big hole you could put your hand through – but I recovered quite quickly. However, I didn't get any kind of artificial leg until after Christmas, and when I did, it had an ordinary round rubber heel on the bottom. It was folded up and made of very strong fibre – and you could walk – but it was like walking with a peg leg. If you sat down on the bus, this wooden leg stuck right out – nobody could get past. People had to step over it, or you would have to get up.

Then I went to Roehampton, which was the hospital for other ranks, while the place for officers was Dover House. It was there that I first had a bath in a millionaire's bathroom! It was beautiful, with blue water – I can see it now – and the loo was like a throne and had arm-rests. There I was measured for an artificial leg – an American leg made by a Swiss firm called Schranz. That was the first proper artificial leg I had.

I got used to it very quickly. I went for the final fitting to get the leg, then I walked from West Kensington to Hammersmith Broadway on it. It chafed like hell, but I was determined to walk on it.

The only thing I could do was to go back into show business. What else did I know? I was only a two-bit actor then, but one thing I'd gained was, from being a two-bit actor to serving as an officer, some rudiments of being an executive – the confidence to give and carry out orders and control the men.

I was in Leeds when I met a bloke called Herbert Darnley. He took me on and for the first time I managed a musical comedy – and I also married the leading lady, Dorothy Fisher. However, I wanted to get a job as a business manager, so I went along in my uniform to meet Herbert Marshall. I'd met him before – he was quite a big star in silent films, and later the talkies – and he'd become a business manager. He thanked me for coming, but said he was sorry he had nothing to offer me – but then as I was leaving, he called out, 'Just wait a minute, Davies. I'm putting on a sketch called "If". Could you manage it?' I said yes, and he told me I could play understudy for the doctor who was understudy for the principal, Herbert Darnley. 'I'll pay you the same as the managers of the touring companies – £15 a week.' I nearly fell through the floor! The most I ever earned in the army was £5 a week as an officer. This was all while I was officially still in the army.

The army told me all they wanted me to do was attend medical boards. I got an offer to appear before a medical board at Caxton Hall, and I wrote back and said it wasn't convenient. I got a letter back that said, 'You are still in the army – you will come back to Caxton Hall for the medical board.' So I did.

Officially I was on sick leave all the time. I then wrote to the War Office resigning my commission. After which I was able to get back to show business as a manager.

Private Horace Astin
4th Battalion, King's Liverpool Regiment

It took me at least six months before I could walk at all – or before I could do anything properly. It takes years to get totally accustomed to having half a limb – you don't get over it straight away. I received my wound in 1918, but I didn't get my limb until 1922, because I had a breakdown. I ended up in hospital several times. I eventually managed to walk – until I broke down completely in 1928.

The problem was something inherent in the wound – something to do with the periosteum – the covering of the bone. Then the infection reached the marrow of the bone and if it had been left, that might have been the end of me, so it had to come off.

I wouldn't say I was bitter about losing my leg – it was one of those things I'd come to expect. I would have much rather have kept it, of course, and it was very, very difficult to come to terms with – but when I saw people without legs and arms I realized I was lucky.

I think after the war I was reasonably treated, according to the rules and regulations. I was discharged with a forty per cent pension – at that time a full pension was £2, so I had sixteen shillings a week.

I've never been one of those people that grunt and grouse about the war – after all, who's to say who's right and who's wrong?

Lloyd Fox

Conscientious objector, served with Friends' Ambulance Unit

In November 1918 I was taken by a young army doctor to a large hall in Courtrai, where we found over a hundred gassed women and children. There they were, with one old lady trying to give them drinks – all terribly affected by the mustard and phosgene gas, which practically destroyed the sight of many of them. Their eyes were very swollen and they couldn't see. Their breathing was also starting to deteriorate, because the phosgene affected the lungs. The object of our visit was to pick out about twenty suitable cases for treatment at the convent – people who would benefit from more experienced nursing treatment. The army doctor took me round the ward and when we got to the end he said, 'I can do nothing – it's up to you. You pick out twenty of these gassed people here, that you think may have some chance of living, and take them up to the convent.'

There was I, a youngster, given what seemed to be the opportunity of saving the lives of twenty people. All I could do was pick twenty of the toughest looking children. I thought they might have some chance of survival. I took them to the convent where they had a special gas unit, but I don't think it was very effective. I remember the following day seeing one of the gas orderlies come out of the ward in tears. He said, 'I can't stand it in there any longer. They're just choking to death, and they're mostly the children you brought in two days ago. Go and see for yourself what it's like.' I went in and there were these unfortunate children, black in the face. Practically nothing could be done for them. In all there were some 800 killed by the gas at that time, and it passed more or less unnoticed. It was a great responsibility to leave some 80 women and children to die with nobody to look after them. But there it was – there were practically no civilians left in Courtrai then. We washed their eyes out with bicarbonate of soda, and the special squad tried bleeding them, but I rather fancy that was a complete waste of time.

Private Jim Fox
11th Battalion, Durham Light Infantry

I now have chest trouble and lots of problems with my eyes since I came out of the army. I used to wake up and my eyes would be blocked with matter as a result of the gas. I wouldn't be able to open them until they were bathed properly with warm water. I used to go to see specialists of all sorts to try to get this cured. Ultimately, after two or three years, I did get it reasonably fixed, but I've always had chest trouble. I said to the doctor that this was due to my experience in the army, and he said, 'It hasn't killed you yet, has it?' It hadn't – but it certainly didn't do me any good!

Private Harry Wells
23rd Battalion, Royal Fusiliers

I owe a lot to the hospital, who did very well for me. I nearly lost my sight from the gas, but luckily I was sent to Le Treport and they dealt with my eyes straight away. I had to bathe my eyes in salt water every day for a year – and then I had to wear a green shade over my eyes for another year and a half before I could stand ordinary daylight. Even now, the sun takes my sight right away, and they say I'm colour-blind too, all as a result of the gas.

When I was blinded immediately after the attack, I always hoped I'd get my sight back. It gave me hope to be having the daily treatment – but I realized that some men were permanently blinded. It all depended on how much damage there was – whether any liquid went into the eyes – because this could happen through explosions or from clothing. Luckily for me I was able to see within a year. I could go to a cinema and see the films! In the sunlight I wore dark glasses and in the evening I wore yellow-tinted driving glasses that turn all white lights amber.

I was convalescing in England and was moved from Dover to Eastbourne – and that was when the effects of the gas started to tell on my chest and lungs – and I still had an open wound that hadn't healed. I wouldn't say I was in pain, but I was constantly uncomfortable. The wound was in my side and was very sore so they wrapped round what they called a 'butterfly lariat' bandage all round my body, with padding inside to kill the pain. I had this bandage on for two years. I suppose I might not have done it any good by going ballroom dancing – but I was still a bachelor, and although I was bandaged up, I would still go dancing.

We used to go dancing in a group together every night in Eastbourne, at Hampden Park and other local places. One night we had been dancing for some time and one girl said, 'Phew! Is there a hospital around here?' I was perspiring, and I suppose that the smell of the wound treatment was seeping out in the heat. In spite of the wound, I enjoyed myself.

The problem was that the infection in my wound came from the inside. The flesh started rotting from the inside, and one lung was collapsed, and a piece of broken rib was breaking through, so they had to keep the wound open to allow the poison to drain. They didn't dare wash it out and seal it up – that would have killed the lung and me along with it. The poison had to find a way out somewhere, so the wound was washed out with Lysol twice a day using a high-pressure spray, because they didn't have antibiotics at that time. This would smart like anything and they would burn away the old flesh at the side of the wound to keep it open – which again used to hurt a lot. The young nurses used to do it – but there was one girl who took a special interest in me, and I think she saved my life with her constant care.

That carried on until October 1920, when I went for a final operation at the hospital in Cambridge. The doctors decided to carve the infection out like a piece of cheese and let the tissue grow gradually together, while still rinsing it out with Lysol to kill the infection on the inside. After this operation I was very ill and my mother received a telegram to say she should come to see me for the last time. My mother and her sister came and I remember them sitting beside my bed and talking before I slipped into a coma. About three weeks later I came round and after that I started to get better – I didn't die as I perhaps should have done.

Eventually I was discharged and sent to a sanatorium for a couple of months. Life there didn't suit me so I went home to my mother to finish convalescing. Then, even though I started doing some work, I still had to go for an army medical examination every month until they were satisfied and discharged me properly.

Fortunately the infection didn't return, but I was left very weak. I had to watch my step – and particularly watch my breathing, because the lung could still collapse – but it gradually got better over the years. Strangely, this went on from when I was nineteen until I was about fifty. Suddenly, at fifty years of age, my body seemed to change and I appeared to have recovered completely. The lung had healed itself, but until then I carried on, a semi-invalid. I was discharged with a full disability pension to start with, then gradually this was cut down to twelve bob a week. After that they discharged me with a thirty per cent life pension.

Dorothy Wright
Nurse with Red Cross Voluntary Aid Detachment at St Dunstan's Home for the Blind

All sorts of things were organized for the blind men – every man on arrival was given a watch with a raised dial with Braille spots on it – dominoes were the same, and playing cards. They were all done in Braille and they had a Braille library, and all this network of huts and passages and long corridors, every place they turned off at a corner there was a knob on the rail so they knew where they were.

I remember one of the men coming in to breakfast, absolutely the colour of coffee – dark, unmilked coffee, because he'd shaved with a stick of brown boot polish by mistake – but instead of getting angry or vexed there were peals of laughter from him and everybody else. It was our great joke, and I hardly ever saw any real depression there. There was one chap who was deaf, dumb and blind, and dying of diabetes – we couldn't get anything across to him, but he didn't live long. Not all the men were permanently blind or entirely blind – some were shellshocked blind – one of them recovered just like that – he woke up and could see, but he nearly went mad, because he got worried that it was some vision he was seeing. There was a lot of trouble with him, but he came round eventually – but at first he was terrified.

The blind had the most amazing sense of touch and distance – there were some radiators down the centre of the ward that lay parallel to the feet of the beds on each side. There was one boy who was quite blind who would come into the ward, then would start running and leapfrog over every single one of these radiators, all the way to the top, and he never made a mistake. It used to terrify me!

Captain Bertram Steward
Tank Corps

At the Front, people might be in trenches that were subjected to really heavy shelling, which went on for hours, and nights and days. I've seen people sitting in their dugouts and imagining that the next shell might be the one for them. I've seen their fingers shaking when they lit up a cigarette – and I've known them to go off their heads in the middle of it. I remember one sergeant suddenly saying, 'I think we'll have a cup of tea. Mary, go and put the kettle on,' imagining he was at home. The next day they'd taken him back – he'd gone completely bonkers. The strain of continual bombardment – not just one then another, but continual – that's what people who had never experienced such terror, didn't understand. Everybody who went through that had shellshock – but it manifested itself in different ways.

Rifleman Fred White
10th Battalion, King's Royal Rifle Corps

Us fellows, it took us years to get over it. Years! Long after when you were working, married, had kids, you'd be lying in bed with your wife and you'd see it all before you. Couldn't sleep. Couldn't lie still. Many and many's the time I've got up and tramped the streets till it came daylight. Walking, walking – anything to get away from your thoughts. And many's the time I've met other fellows that were out there doing exactly the same thing. That went on for years, that did.

Dr Michael Yealland
Father treated shellshock patients at the National Hospital for the Paralysed and Epileptic

The patients my father was treating who were diagnosed with shellshock were not only those who had been rather resistant to treatment, but who had gross physical disorders such as paralysis of limbs, deafness, muteism – which still persisted. The problem was that they had just had too much – they could no longer take what they were experiencing and it showed itself in various forms.

With some patients he was able to affect a cure with persuasion or what some might regard as trickery. He said to one patient who was mute, he said to him, 'Your mother wears a wig,' and the patient suddenly blurted out, 'She does not', and after that he was able to talk normally.

Caroline Maud Edgley
Nurse with Red Cross Voluntary Aid Detachment

Families might only come once a month or a fortnight to visit the patients at Knutsford Hospital – although some would come once a week if they didn't live too far away. But mostly it meant a journey they had to pay for themselves, and if they had young children they had to find someone to look after them. On the whole the men didn't seem to mind very much – although naturally they liked to see them – although sometimes it would remind them too much of home.

We didn't have much in the way of occupational therapy then in the wards, and they were in too bad a condition to have physiotherapy. They might have this in the second hospital, for the incurables, to get some use back into a hand, for instance, but still nothing on the scale we have nowadays. They would draw – that was why they liked to draw in somebody's book – it gave them an outlet.

There was a sergeant who was shellshocked. He was a very nice man ordinarily, but he had this obsession about the day he was blown up by a shell, with all his men. He seemed to remember that day, and that he was in charge of these men and had to see to their food. He used to call me every night and ask me to go to the village shop to get some food for his men. He'd say the money was in his locker. I would take the money and go out, and perhaps come back with something or other, and tell him it was in his locker with his change. Then he would be quite content – felt he was looking after his men. That was the sole thing on his mind – he'd ask what had happened to so and so? We would tell him that the man had been moved to another hospital. On one occasion he got very agitated. Perhaps he'd looked in his locker and found there wasn't anything there and thought I'd been playing him up. 'I shan't ask you to do anything for me any more – don't you come near me.' He shouted at me and heaved himself out of bed and took hold of me and just threw me on to the next bed. I kept my distance from him after that. I hoped he'd forget it, and I think he did. He didn't realise after a week or so that I was the same person looking after him. He even accused me once of being a spy.

Annie Esler
Red Cross Voluntary Aid Detachment

There was a mental section of Kings College Hospital, called the Maudsley, which was opposite Kings, and this was where the mental cases went.

We had shellshock patients and they were very difficult to deal with, needing special treatment. I think quite a lot of them went to homes specially for shellshock cases once it was realized how bad they were. You couldn't keep them in with the other men. They used to get very upset and very mentally distressed over their experiences – and a lot of them had brain injuries which were pretty awful.

Private George Grunwell
16th Battalion, West Yorkshire Regiment

When I was shot, it was all so quick. There was a flash, which is the only thing I remember about it. The next thing I knew, I was bleeding down the side of my face and they got me to the field dressing station. I lost consciousness, I was unable to speak and I was paralysed down one side.

I was taken to an intermediate hospital then shipped back to England and to King George's Hospital in London. My main treatment there was compulsory quiet and rest – I was confined to bed and not allowed to get up. My father and one of my brothers came to see me – but living two hundred miles away and in wartime conditions, they didn't come often. Wartime privations were biting at home. Poorer people didn't have money to throw away, and my family couldn't keep paying the fare to London.

I was in hospital about three months, during which time I was improving day by day. While I was there, the Yorkshire Men's Society used to take an interest in any Yorkshiremen who were there, and one day when I was feeling better, they took some of us out to the pantomime.

The Red Cross people used to come round and give us canvas and all the threads to do needlework. They suggested stitching your regimental cap badge. If you did one for them, then you could do one for yourself free of charge. That helped a little to break the monotony of lying in bed, day after day. But eventually I was well enough to convalesce, and they sent me to Kingston-upon-Thames. A group of us went there, and when we were well, we were able to go into the neighbouring village of Surbiton.

My convalescence ended around January, and a group of us returned to the hospital in London. I was discharged from St George's Hospital the following February, and by that time I could walk about a bit. From there we were not demobilized, but discharged as unfit for service. I was pleased to put my war experience behind me, and I was keen to start again in civilian life. I was rigged out with a new set of clothes – a new suit and a trilby hat – and that was the end of it.

They granted me a part-pension for twelve months, after which I had to appear before a board. The pension carried on for a further six months but eventually I appeared before another board and they allocated me a final payment – and that was the end of financial support. I was convinced that the whole objective of the medical boards was to get you off their backs, with regard to money, as soon as they could.

My initial payment was twenty-five shillings, and the pension for total disablement was then £2. All the time I was receiving a pension, I was still hampered by my injuries – but otherwise I was reasonably well.

At the time I didn't think my injury had caused any permanent damage, but I wonder now, when I get a pain in my head from time to time, whether it's a direct result of that explosion.

I wasn't awarded any special medals – just the general service ones. The experience of those four years in the army seemed to count for nothing. I also received a silver badge when I was discharged 'with honour for services rendered', which I suppose was of some value.

If you were discharged with the war still on, it was useful to have the badge, so that people who saw you understood. Once I was on leave from France, and a lad who was older than me and who had joined up got a severe shrapnel wound. He was taken back to hospital as quickly as possible, and eventually he had to have a silver plate put in his head. He was, 'Discharged no further use'. When I came on leave, he came to the station to meet me. As we were crossing the station forecourt we heard some people saying, 'Why isn't he in the army?' I just said to them, 'That young man has been in the army. He was wounded in the head and he has a plate in it.' So I felt it was only right to let people see and understand.

Sister Nell Brink
US Base Hospital No 27 (University of Pittsburgh)

I was nursing the wounded French soldiers in Dr Blake's hospital on the Rue Puccini in Paris, and my favourite was Boillose – nineteen years old, right leg and left arm amputated. He had black hair and red rosy cheeks.

I went down to the Medical Chief and told him it was my last day in the hospital, and said, 'I just have one ambition before I leave. I'd like to take my Boillose for a walk in the Bois – take him down to Rumpelmeyers, the famous tea salon – I think it would be a nice treat for him.' The staff were all delighted – anything I could do for a Frenchman.

I went downstairs and got the wheelchair, put him in it and took him out. He was not overenthusiastic, but he was satisfied. They were so used to accepting, the French, after four years. They were pretty stoical, but he had had so many operations that just the odour of ether alone, while going through the hospital corridor, would turn him pale and sick.

In the Bois it was lovely. The French people saw us in American uniforms and gave him a flower and put it in his buttonhole.

Then I called a taxi and we went to Rumpelmeyers and it was the nicest place in the world!

I didn't know what to order for Boillose, because I'm no drinker myself, so I ordered a long champagne drink, full of fruit. It was nice for the occasion. We had that and we took our time, and the waitress came over and was so nice to him, and after tea we went back in another taxi.

He enjoyed it in his own way, I suppose, but he didn't say very much. Very stoical. Didn't smile or anything. I took him back to his ward and said, '*Au revoir*'. We were sleeping on the top floor in the same building where we were nursing, so after I'd packed my things I went down and there he was, sitting in a chair in the middle of the ward, surrounded with his Frenchmen, and he was telling them the whole story. They were having a real gay time.

Angela Limerick
Nurse with Volunteer Aid Detachment

There wasn't the advanced plastic surgery in those days that we have now, but Dr Harold Gillies did great work in the First World War at St Mary's Hospital, Sidcup, and he was father-in-law to McIndoe, who carried on the work in the Second World War. He started developing plastic surgery, which made such an enormous difference to those facially scarred men.

With the surgical cases, some of them were immobilized for a very long time – they had legs in traction and couldn't be moved. The average stay was longer than it would be now with all the sophisticated treatments available – now they get them up more quickly. I don't think our men were ever pushed to get up immediately after an operation, but today the poor wretch would be put on his feet at once. The anaesthetics were very largely ether – there was none of this comforting treatment of being given an injection before being taken down to the theatre so you don't know what's going on. The patients were just wheeled into the theatre and given their anaesthetic on the spot – with the sight of all these torture implements around them. The surgeons just got on with the job as quickly as possible – and the patients were awfully sick when they came round.

The patients used to play games to pass the time. They would chat with each other and read, and play dominoes and whist. They had a gramophone – often there was one each end of the ward, both playing different tunes. They didn't have a day room – and in winter they were only too glad to sit round the ward stove, wrapped in blankets. They were very self-sufficient – they just amused themselves. I don't think anyone did any crafts, but they used to write in each other's albums. One patient made a wonderful musical instrument out of an old box and some bits of wire – it was a bit like a guitar – and they used to sing a lot.

Edith Cecily Evans
Nurse with Red Cross Voluntary Aid Detachment

I was still working in the hospital six months after the war. It was a difficult time – I think the medical cases were more inclined to be depressed – but we all knew the end was coming and we just lived for that. We didn't know what date we were going to close down – but we closed on the first of April 1919. After the men had gone, we nurses and the local people had a bit of a party, and some of the airmen managed to come back, and we danced 'til daylight. But I've never forgotten the day the last lot of men went back to Sharncliffe, and there were no patients left in the hospital. I went into the bathroom and found a cigarette lying on the windowsill – the one thing I had been training them never to do – and I burst into tears. It was the end, and I wouldn't see them any more.

Mrs I McNicol
Civilian

My husband only got home after the end of the war, and he was so ill. Malaria. He was in the Scottish Horse, and he'd been in Gallipoli and Egypt. I hadn't seen him for four years. My little girl was three and a bit and he'd never seen her. He came home straight off a hospital ship and he was so weary and unwell and went straight to bed. I said to Connie, 'Go in and see your daddy.' She was very shy of him, but she went and stood at the bedroom door. I said, 'Well, say something to Daddy.' She said, 'My Mummy's made scones for you.' He just looked at her. He was too ill, too tired to speak. We lived with my family for a while. We'd had a war wedding before he left, so we didn't have a house of our own. After a few months we were given a railway carriage to live in. That was the 'Home for Heroes'. It was the best they could do. So we started our married life in a converted railway carriage.

May Brooks
Civilian

I saw sights that turned me against the war. We lived in Kingston-on-Thames, almost in Richmond at that time, and we'd just got married. The Star and Garter home for disabled men was there, and one evening we were walking past, just as a coachload of soldiers – disabled men – came by. I shall never forget it. Some had got no legs, some were blind, and I remember saying to my husband, 'Well, if that's war . . .' That's the first real thing that I'd seen – a mass of the results of the war, and it made me think what a terrible thing it was. They were young – yet they were ruined for life.

Private Ernie Rhodes
16th Battalion, Manchester Regiment

I was back at home and out of the army, and one day I was on a tram when suddenly my shoulder dislocated, and I had to go to hospital. For twelve years I was in and out of hospital. None of the doctors could fix it. They would pull it about until it jumped in again – but I went through hell for years. There was a problem with my knee too. They measured my leg and I had lost an inch and a half below and an inch above my knee. So they gave me some electric treatment to stop it getting any smaller. I thought I might well lose my leg, and what with my shoulder playing me up, I thought I'd put in for a pension – but they turned me down. They asked if I had any proof of need!

I told them exactly what happened and my former corporal sent them a report. He wrote down exactly what injuries I'd received during the war, and eventually I got awarded a thirty per cent disability pension. Then, within a week or so, I'd just got home from work, and my mum says, 'There's a letter from the pensions people,' and these are the very words – and let's not forget, I went to France twice, and I was only a boy when I was conscripted – 'We have overruled a decision arrived at in Manchester. We have found that your injuries are neither caused nor brought on by your army service.' God strike me dead if that is a lie! That made me very bitter.

Private William Holmes
12th Battalion, London Regiment

When I got back to England from the Front I was discharged as being unfit for further service. The bullet that struck me was still lodged, and they gave me a disability pension of 7/6 a week. This pension lasted for two years, then they cut it off – until one day my brother John said to me, 'In the *Express* today, it says that chaps who've had their pensions knocked off can go before an appeal board.' So I applied to the appeal board in Chelsea and was given an appointment. When I went to see them, there were seven doctors who examined me. Straight away, they said, 'We're not going to bother with the army x-rays – we're sending you directly to a private x-ray doctor.'

The private doctor had an enormous x-ray machine – and two days later I received a copy of the letter which he had sent to the pensions people. In it he said, 'I have x-rayed this man today, and found the bullets where he complains of pains – and also metallic filings in four different places.' Some time later my wife took one of those metal filings out of my left arm with tweezers – and they took another piece out of me at the Ramsgate Hospital.

I had been seeing a doctor because I'd hurt my ankle, and while the doctor was checking that, I said, 'It feels to me as if I have got a tooth stuck in the back of my throat.' He said, 'Open your mouth.' He shone the torch into my mouth and said, 'You've got something there I have never seen before. I'll give you a note and I want you to go straight down to Ramsgate Hospital.' He sent me to see an ear, nose and throat surgeon who asked me to keep perfectly still, then with his scalpel, he cut into the back of my throat. He used his tweezers and pulled out a mass of debris, including some metallic filings. He called a nurse and said, 'Bet you've never seen anything like this!'

I've still got one piece in my head that's been there some sixty-five years now. Even so, my health was never too bad, even with a bullet left in me. I never had any sickness.

However, I couldn't go back to my old job at the Army and Navy Store – that was fine while I was living in London – but when I got married, we moved to Broadstairs, because my wife's sister gave us a house there, with all the furniture. All we had to pay was £2 a week for the mortgage. In Broadstairs we earned a living quite differently. My wife is a very good watercolour artist, and I got a peddler's license from the police for door-to-door selling – and I'd sell the birthday cards she painted – for which I charged sixpence each. People would buy half a dozen at a time, to use until I came around next time. I was making not a bad living from all my rounds. At Christmas time she'd paint 1500 Christmas cards, and the first week of September I'd go all around Margate and Ramsgate, taking up orders to keep us busy right up to Christmas.

Private Thomas Peck

23rd Battalion, Royal Fusiliers

I had to undergo several medicals, and eventually I was put on a pension – it was £1 a week for several weeks, then the next time I went to the medical board they reduced it, and the third time I appeared, they asked me to walk across the floor and back. I just walked across and back as normally as I could – although I could have put on a limp. They measured me up and I was about half an inch shorter in one leg than the other. The doctor asked what had happened, and I said I'd caught a sniper's bullet. On the paper it said that the femoral artery had been divided, but he replied that if the femoral artery had been divided, I'd be an angel. Eventually he said, 'We're going to finish your case by giving you a lump sum. It won't be enough to get you a motor car.' In the event, I got about £40 – which was nothing in those days. I should have fought for more.

I used to play a lot of sport – especially football – but my days of sport were finished from the day I got wounded, and I got no compensation for all that. I could have fought against it after-wards, but I never joined the British Legion, who might have taken the case up for me.

If you lost a finger you got a pension for life, and if you were disfigured you got something. I was just thankful to think I could walk. So why worry?

Gunner William Towers
Royal Field Artillery

After I had my leg amputated if I met up with some colleagues I always went out for a drink or two. Before I was courting, every night when I was at home, somebody would come to meet me and we would go down to town to a pub to meet the troops. I was still in the army and I had the same money as them.

At the time we were on rations, and there was a place in the centre of Leeds I was advised to go to. I heard that I was entitled to more rations and they sent me on to a place in Quebec Street. I went along, and there were all these ladies running it. 'Now, how can I help you?' 'Could I have some rations please?' 'What would you like, love? Would you like some butter?' 'Oh, yes.' 'How much? Two pounds?' I took my father down with me and I got two pounds of this and two pounds of that. We went away with a whole kit-bag full. It turned out that those coming back on leave and the disabled could go and get special rations. Oh, that was good!

One of the things that BLESMA did was to look after people's welfare – there were old men who were very poor, and they tried to sort out their pensions. Although I was discharged in 1919, I never got the full pension due to me until I retired.

The pension due to you when you have had a leg amputated is worked out by how far up your thigh they've cut – so they measure from the top down. When you first have the amputation your leg is fat, so the flesh sags down below where the bone is cut. They took a slide rule to my stump and measured to just touch the flesh. Now, if that measurement comes below mid-thigh you only got a sixty per cent disability pension. But on me, if they'd pressed it up to touch the bone it would have been above mid-thigh – but they didn't, so they gave me just sixty per cent at first.

Eventually I appealed against this. They sent me the other side of Leeds to where nobody knew me, to have a doctor check my stump. He got all the paperwork, and I said, 'You are to measure the thigh bone of my good leg, and then from the top to the end of the bone on the stump. If what's left is under half the measurement, I get a seventy per cent pension, but if it's over, I get sixty per cent.' He measured and said that it was well under. He sent off his report, and several weeks later I got a letter asking me to see another doctor at a different address, somewhere else in Leeds, where I wasn't known. This second doctor measured me and came up with the same result. I then got a letter from London saying 'there will be no further correspondence, and this matter is now closed'. That was the end, and I couldn't do a thing about it. That was around 1935. It was after that I started working with BLESMA.

BLESMA used to deal with pensions too, and I told the welfare fellow about my problem He contacted a solicitor in the head office in London who took my details and he referred my case to a medical board for war pensions. They agreed that I should have got the seventy per cent – although I still couldn't have back pay. They would only backdate it from the time when the BLESMA welfare man put in an appeal. They gave me £1000 back pay, but it should have been £6,000 to £7,000 – after all, I'd done forty-two years at ten per cent a week too little. That made me feel bitter, but when I was working I didn't mind as long as I got my pay each week.

Overall, since losing my leg, there's been good and bad. Pensions-wise I really feel they robbed me – but with regard to housing I didn't do badly as I got a corporation house. I enjoyed life after that. I don't want to die now – I can say I have enjoyed life since, and I have enjoyed helping others – it has been my whole life.

Private K Hares
Oxfordshire and Buckinghamshire Light infantry

'I am directed by the Ministry of Health to inform you that your degree of disability is now too small to entitle you to any further award. You have therefore been awarded a final gratuity of £27 10 shillings, which will be paid to you when the temporary pension you are drawing expires.'

So that was the sum I had. That was summer of 1920, and ever since then I have suffered from poor health. Although I was never a gas casualty, I was in a sector where gas shells were used, and I must have had a whiff of it. When I was working in London, much later in 1933, I went to St Thomas' Hospital. They'd never had a case like mine before. The only thing they could do in those days was treatment using a long rubber tube, about the size of an ordinary gas pipe, loaded with mercury to give it weight. This was passed down through the gullet to break a contraction that formed on the weight of the stomach. I had that daily for many, many years. I still carried on with my work, but I had to be a bit careful with eating, because that could get a bit difficult.

When I went home to Weston-super-Mare looking for a job they didn't want to know about me – they couldn't give a damn. They only had council houses for key workers, and I thought to myself, 'What the hell have I been all this time, then?' We weren't key workers, apparently after all we'd been through. The British public never realized or appreciated what myself and all the other fellows had experienced.

Private J W Emerson
Northumberland Fusiliers

I was discharged just before the end of the war and got a forty per cent disability pension. When I got home, all my mates were away in the army and I didn't want to go back to the pit – so I went to Newcastle and joined the Northumberland Fusiliers. I camouflaged my wounds and said I was fit, and when asked if I'd been in the army before, I told them I'd been working in the pit. I was only in the Northumberland Fusiliers for three weeks when the last great battle in France was raging, and we were rushed on to the boat – before I knew where I was, I was back in France again fighting against the Germans.

When the war finished they sent us to Dieppe, where everybody was rushing to get their ticket back – but I wasn't bothered. Dieppe wasn't bad and I was put on the dock police in charge of a Chinese Labour Corps who were waiting to go home. Eventually I came up for my medical board and they said they were in a queer predicament with me. Back home there was a pension building up for me, and in France I was the fittest man in the regiment. They asked me what I wanted to do, and so I said that if it was worth my while, I'd soldier on. They offered me £90, but I asked for £120 – I decided that if they said yes, I'd stay on. That was what happened, and I soldiered on for another twelve months. By this time they were decreasing numbers, and I was told I might as well go home.

I came back, and went back to the pits – however, within two years of being back, I joined the Durham Light Infantry and was back in harness again.

Sapper George Clayton
175 Tunnelling Company, Royal Engineers

I was discharged by the medical board because of the state of my heart, and I was given a pension of forty per cent. In those days you had to go every year to a medical board to be reassessed. When I first went up I got away with it and continued on a forty per cent pension for the following year, but when I went the next time, it was reduced to thirty per cent – then when I went again they reduced it to twenty-five per cent. When the time came around to go for another medical examination, I thought I'd have to do something. I told them I was suffering from heart trouble, so they asked me how defective my heart was. I told them that when I climbed the hill I get short of breath – in fact it was troubling me even when walking. It affected me when I lifted anything heavy too. All the same, they reduced my pension to twenty per cent, but it was set at that for life, so after that I didn't have to attend medical boards any more.

I think my heart is better now than it was then – because it gives you real shock when a shell bursts near you. I once had a shell drop at my feet, but it didn't explode – otherwise there would have been nothing left of me – just pieces of cloth and some raw meat.

Lieutenant Ernest Millard
Royal Field Artillery

I was with my father's business before I joined up, and I went back immediately I was demobbed. I was an apprentice in the printing factory and represented the firm outside. By this time I was only twenty-one, but I felt I was quite an old man after the war. I had been under quite a lot of shelling, and although I wasn't evacuated due to shell shock, I wasn't far from it. I think I was pretty unsettled and restless, and I would have found it difficult to sit down at a desk for any length of time.

I felt very sympathetic towards men who suffered from shell-shock, because these fellows quite simply lost their nerve and ran – and they were taken from the lines and they were shot, for the simple reason that if one man runs, then others would follow. I had absolutely no doubt that shell shock existed – I have seen fit, strong men shaking like leaves and I had a lot of sympathy for them. The fact was, that their nerves went. For myself, my nerve hadn't gone, but I'd found the experience of shelling very unsettling – it certainly took its toll. I suppose we felt that in the course of a year in action, we had lost a lot of our youth.

I came under gas attack too, but my eyesight is fine – absolutely clear. But it's a very curious thing that, after the gassing, I found myself prone to passing out without warning – I'd suddenly faint. One night, back home, I was in a restaurant and I felt myself going. I got upstairs, didn't lock the door and I passed out. There was a doctor in the restaurant, who came out to see me, and he said, 'You've been gassed haven't you?' He knew from the colour of my face. I passed out on a bus, and in the train – all sorts of places – quite frequently, but it gradually got less and less. I still have no idea of the reason for it.

Even after the gas, my chest was absolutely fine – luckily I have been extremely fit all my life. But there was an upside to my experiences in the war – I learnt the values of everything – human beings in particular. In my work, before I went into the army, I was with the men on the factory floor – I understood those men, and when I went to the battery, they recognized that I understood them, and I got complete co-operation.

Once I got back to my father's works, I never stayed in the factory – I was on the outside as a rep. I settled down to that pretty well, and I had an easy time for a year, then I settled back into full-time work.

Private Francis Sumpter
17th Field Ambulance, RAMC

On January 26th 1921, it was no surprise to me to be up before a medical board. My arm had been useless for years. The thing wouldn't dry up and heal properly. The medical board declared me thirty per cent disabled and gave me a disabled pension –

which was taken away in 1922, because although I was disabled by army standards, according to the civilian grading, I wasn't. By civilian standards, I had full use of my wounded arm because I could move it. They gave me two years at eight shillings a week, and then a final pay-off. I asked them why they thought my condition would be better in two years' time, and they said, 'It doesn't have to get better. You have got full movement there.' I explained that I couldn't go back into my former work in the bespoke shoe trade. I'd need to have two arms fully working – and my one arm was useless. So they said they'd give me training, and they sent me to a government factory in Tottenham to train as a tailor. Just try picking up a piece of cloth and putting a needle through when you can only use one arm! The man in charge – a former major – said, 'You're no use as a tailor – you can't hold a garment. You won't be able to sew. I will give you a test. Try to make a buttonhole, and if you can't do that, we'll have to do something else for you.' So I tried to make a buttonhole – I knew how to, but I couldn't do it. I couldn't hold the cloth still to get the needle through. He said, 'You can stay on here – see the system of how a garment is made, and I'll show you the cutting room. You've got two years to stay here – but you can probably become a foreman once you know your job.' So I carried on and got to know all about how the job was done in the cutting room, how a garment was mocked up and chalked up; then baste-stitched – and eventually I knew the job from start to finish.

I was sent out to find an employer – and was told that whoever employed me would get half my wages. The first factory I went to was Simpsons-in-the-Strand, whose factory was in Stoke New-ington. They said, 'You want to be a foreman? What training have you done?' I told them about the last two years, but they said, 'You've never worked anywhere – so you've never had any experience?' I said, 'No – not practical experience.' He said, 'Answer me this. If I gave you half a dozen three-piece jobs, how many coat hands, waistcoat hands and trouser hands would you need?' I said I didn't know, and he said, 'There you are – we couldn't trust our production hands to you. Go and look for something else. You'll never get a job in sewing unless you are experienced. There are plenty of experienced foreman tailors out of work who shouldn't be working in factories. What you've learned isn't of much use to you.'

Sybil Morrison
Pacifist and ambulance driver in London

I grew up in a very Tory environment, with servants and what have you. I must have been rather a rebel because in 1911, when I was eighteen, I joined the Women's Social and Political Union. It was Mrs Pankhurst's organization in the struggle for women getting the vote. I have one sister, older than me, but while she was not unsympathetic to my ideas, she was much more conventional and she got married and had children – grand-children now. Her husband fought in the First World War and was gassed and shellshocked. When he came home, hardly sur-prisingly, he couldn't get a job, and he eventually committed suicide in 1928. I have always thought of him as a war casualty.

It was very upsetting for the people coming home. My brother-in-law had been an estates agent to Lord Carrington, who had promised to keep his job open. When the last of the family died, someone else came in, and there was no job left for him. For these men coming home, going around the labour exchanges was one of the horrors of the First World War. A home fit for heroes to live in – and they couldn't live in it.

Mrs Pankhurst threw down everything and went to the war – and so did I. But I think we were conned – we were meant to believe that this was a war to end all wars and there would never be another one. I don't know how I could have been so foolish as to believe that, because my intelligence tells me that you can't end wars by using wars. But we believed it – oh, we certainly believed it.

The truly awful thing was the people who were killed – the slaughter that was going on – and the terrible knock on the door with the telegram saying, 'We regret to inform you that your son has been killed in action'. I think it is because of this slaughter of all this generation of young men that we – my generation – think they were so wonderful. They were all beautiful creatures to us and I think back to my young cousins and my friends – they all seem so wonderful, and it is only because they died so young, before their time. We commemorated them with all these little shrines that sprung up all over the country.

There were really tragic events. I had one cousin – he was very young and an only child and he joined up when he was really too young. He had to get permission from his parents – who of course really didn't want him to learn to fly. He was only a kid, I can see him now, so pleased with his big fur gloves – and they wore their little hats on the side of their heads, the little forage caps that the fliers wore in those days. He was always sweeping back a floppy lock of his hair which naturally blew about... He hadn't been gone more than a few days when he was shot down. We learned that he'd been killed when they sent back all his uniform without warning. This is one of the things the Germans were nice about in that war – they seemed to care about the airmen and where they buried them, and they put up little sticks over their graves so that later they could be moved into proper graveyards – but it was all very unpleasant really.

At home we heard about what it was like when the men came back on leave – though they were pretty unwilling to talk about it. They just wanted to forget it. Many were brought back to hospital – my brother-in-law was in Guy's Hospital after he was gassed. He couldn't speak for a very long time, but when he could speak he was quite prepared to tell us what was going on. I think we had a lot of information first-hand.

It's always been said that women got the vote because of what we did in the war. I can assure you this is not true. The vote was given to women of thirty and over. Well, I wasn't thirty when the war came to an end. I'd been twenty-one when it broke out and I was twenty-five or twenty-six when it finished. Women of thirty got the vote – and they had to be householders. So it was all nonsense, it was a very limited vote. We didn't really get it until 1928 when Baldwin gave what was called the 'Flapper Vote'. They'd always had denigrating words for women. However the Flapper Vote didn't work for Baldwin – in fact he was out. He made a mistake in thinking that women would vote for him. I know women did a great deal in the First World War – they were conscripted to do it in the Second World War but they did it voluntarily and willingly in the First. It all seemed so much more romantic to be told that you were fighting for the cause, in a war to end all wars.

Among my relations, the fact that their sons, my cousins, had been killed didn't make them sympathetic to conscientious objection – although I feel it ought to have. But there was this attitude, 'I have given my son', which always upset me – because nobody has the right to 'give' somebody else and I think on the whole they did go willingly. Conscription didn't come in until 1916 so that really the very best of our young people were killed off by 1916 and people had stopped going gladly to join up.

The 'No More War' movement came into existence after the First World War. There was a No-Conscription Fellowship too. Women couldn't actually be full members of the movement, because they couldn't go to prison as conscientious objectors, but women certainly helped out in the background.

I really had no idea until much later after the war that there were so many people who wanted to join these groups – I was very surprised when I discovered how many there were. I had a school friend who was engaged to be married to a conscientious objector, and she had a very hard time really because people did disapprove of it. They thought it was terrible.

In that war we didn't have any figurehead as terrible as Hitler, so for people who went to war against the Kaiser, they had to build them up an image that the Kaiser was as bad as a madman. I think you have to get people worked up before you can go to war. I simply don't think that war is the right way at all to settle anything. It's such a gamble – and a gamble with humans' lives. That's why I am a pacifist, and I haven't ever looked back at all.

Harold Bing
Conscientious objector

On the 8th April 1919, all those conscientious objectors who'd been in prison more than two years were set free. Those who had not, remained in prison and were released as and when they reached the two years mark. By the end of summer all remaining prisoners had been released.

When the war had been over for some months the general public ceased to be hostile on the whole and was just indifferent, and therefore the government could yield to the pressure of the sympathetic among the public without offending the others. During the wartime they could not possibly have done so. There would have been an outcry if conscientious objectors were released while other people's sons were still in the trenches – one can quite understand that.

My father had had to face a certain amount of criticism at work. At one point when all the Post Office staff was required to take an oath of allegiance, he declined to do so except with written reservation. The postmaster tried to persuade him. Father never got any further promotion after that. Younger men with a good military record who would certainly, as everybody agreed, never have received promotion but for the fact that my father was barred from further promotion, were promoted over him. That continued – he never reached any higher grade as a result of having adopted a pacifist attitude during the war.

I was lucky in having a sympathetic family behind me. Some had very hostile families. Some marriages broke down because the wife could not accept the husband's position. A man whose wife was unsympathetic and who probably was not getting enough to live on and maintain children, would be worrying the whole time about his wife and family.

After my discharge I received from the Regimental Paymaster, a money order for two shillings, with a note saying this sum was due to me. I was amused and kept the money order. After about a month I received a further letter from the Paymaster saying that he couldn't trace that it had been cashed and as it was now expired, if I would send it back to him he would send me another one – which I thought was very generous. I simply replied that I was keeping it as a souvenir and no intention of cashing it. How I managed to earn two shillings I don't know! There must have been some day when I wasn't given an order and therefore didn't disobey – that's the only thing I can imagine. That was one day's pay for a private soldier in those days. On my discharge certificate, he had put me down as belonging to the 5th Northern Company, Non-Combatants Corps. So I sent it back, just for a joke, saying, 'This is wrong!' I was supposed to be attached to the 9th Eastern Non-Combatant Corps. Again I had a very polite letter, sending me the discharge certificate saying, 'It's quite in order, Mr Bing. While you were in prison, 9th Eastern Company was demobilized, and in order to avoid demobilizing you, we transferred you to another unit which wasn't demobilized.' They were going to let us out before time, so for the latter part, apparently, I was attached to the 5th Northern Company – although I didn't know it. There's a discharge certificate which threatens me with two years' imprisonment with hard labour if I attempted to join the army. The warder said to me, 'With all the old crooks I've known,

I thought I knew all the tricks – but you conscientious objectors have taught me some new ones.'

A GENERATION LOST

While the men were at the Front, their numbers were steadily eroded by the attrition of war, then in 1918 by the ravages of 'flu. The concern foremost in the minds of those at home was the enormous loss to individual families across the nation. Hardly a family had remained untouched. So great were the losses, however, that the balance of population in the years after the war was tragically upset. There were simply not enough men of marriageable age, in sound health, to provide husbands for a whole generation of young women. With not enough men to go round, the less-than-attractive or socially disadvantaged girls faced a solitary future.

Rosamund Essex
Seventeen-year-old schoolgirl in Bournemouth

Only one out of every ten of my friends has ever married. Quite simply, there were no men available. We had to face the fact that our lives would be stunted in one direction. We should never have the kind of happy homes in which we ourselves had been brought up. There would be no husband, no children, no sexual outlet, no natural bond of man and woman. It was going to be a struggle indeed.

Rose Harrison

Working in service as a lady's maid

Marriage was the goal of every woman servant. It wasn't easy for them. After the war men were scarce, the demand far outweighed the supply and a maid's limited and irregular time off was an added disadvantage. Then there was the having to be back by ten o'clock, which made every date like Cinderella's ball – only you didn't lose your slipper – you could lose your job. There was no status in being a servant – you were a nobody; marriage was the only way out of it.

Amy Gomm

Working in a haberdashers

One day in 1920, I opened my wages bag and found a note telling me I only had one week to go with the firm. The respite I'd enjoyed was explained by the fact that there was no man home from the war with an actual claim on a job in our shop. Those who had left didn't return to it. Tragically, in some cases they couldn't.

So the decision-makers had let it ride. Mass unemployment now forced their hands. There were men – married men with family responsibilities – begging for work. They couldn't justify keeping girls on. The job was – always had been – a man's.

Every cloud has a silver lining. We no longer had to spend our evenings and weekends doing the chores. We had a domestic help living in – me.

Kathleen Gibb
Civilian

I was engaged to a dear boy who joined up when he was eighteen and came through, as we thought at the time, without a scratch. He used to tell me about his life in the trenches – Passchendaele, the Somme, Mons. Some time after, my fiancé was taken ill, then recovered, but the illness recurred and was diagnosed as consumption, or tuberculosis. Then the doctors realized it was caused through being gassed twice during the conflict, it had eaten away one lung and was affecting the other. At that time there was no cure for TB. He died after four years – just faded away. I was broken hearted. He had no war pension as it was too late to apply. When I think, I could have been a happy grandmother today if it hadn't been for that terrible war.

John Dray
One of 8 children, whose father suffered injuries with Northamptonshire Regiment

My father received a wound which was sufficiently bad to bring him back to England. He came back in early 1916, but was sent back to the Front early in 1917. My mother swears that at that time the wound in his shoulder was still weeping.

They decided to send the Northants up to the Ypres Salient where there was going to be a major attack. They crossed the Bellevarde Ridge, and as they were going over, a shell burst and buried him. My father had been hit in the head, with another piece of shrapnel in his body. He was also suffering from shellshock, so they sent him back to England. He was treated in a military hospital near Woolwich, where the walking wounded were allowed out. My mother said that if there was a German air raid, our ack-ack guns would be firing and the nurses would have to hold my father down because of his terror of being under bombardment. The shellshock was quite severe, and even a car back-firing would make him jump. However, he got over it and they discharged him just before the war ended. He had a silver badge and his three medals – Pip, Squeak and Wilfred, as they called them.

He went back to work on the Woolwich Ferry, and became Deputy Pier Master. I was born in 1926, and when I was two, he came home from work before Christmas, and he said to my mother, 'I've got a headache, I think I'll go to bed.' He went to bed, and my sister went up with a cup of tea for him. She came running down and said there was something funny with Daddy's eye. My mother said his eye was bulging out on one side. They rushed him in to hospital in an ambulance. It was a blood clot, which was pushing on the eye from behind, so they removed his eye altogether. They thought that was the end, and he'd be 'One-eyed George' for the rest of his life – but the next day, Christmas Eve, which was also my mother's birthday, the blood clot came back. That night she went up to the hospital with my father's mother. They chatted to him but he was very dozy. Then he suddenly became clear. He said, 'Elsie, have you hung the children's stockings up?' She said, 'Not yet.' So he said, 'Go home and do that, and I'll see you tomorrow.' And before she got home he was dead. The blood clot had touched the brain and had killed him.

My mother was six months pregnant with my youngest sister at the time, so by March there were eight of us. She had some very good friends where we lived in New Eltham, and there were some quite affluent people around – members of the church – who were generous to my mother in that they gave her things for us children and presents for us at Christmas – but that didn't go on for long. My father hadn't been working long enough for the Woolwich Ferry to justify a pension, but she had a lump sum of £400 paid her – which was quite a lot of money really. The amount widows got for children was very small – ten shillings for the widow, five shillings for the oldest child and 2/6 for each of the others – so it didn't even come to two pounds. She had a couple of bachelor brothers who were always telling her how to bring up her children, and she got fed up with this. In 1931 she decided to move and bring us up in the country.

Bombardier William Blundy
Royal Artillery

After the war we searched all the cemeteries everywhere for my brother Albert's grave. I saw on television that there were 307 people shot for cowardice – but I was sure my brother wouldn't have been shot for being a coward – he wasn't a coward.

We even saw the place where they used to shoot the people – 'cowards' they called them. Three hundred and seven were shot in the first war, for cowardice because they wouldn't fight. I wouldn't like to judge them. Who am I to say? I didn't have to go over the top with a gun and bayonet to try to kill people. I just fired the guns – that's all I did.

The place where they shot them was a long shed made of corrugated iron. One night, when we were being moved from one part to another, we saw this shed and went to see what it was used for, because it was empty. We saw this big post fixed in the ground – they used to tie the man to this post with a strap, then shoot him in the back of the head.

Sergeant B W Carmichael
Royal Welch Regiment

I was not too pleased when Captain Rudge told me that I was to be promoted – which meant I would not have to stay on to sort things out to take back to England. It was then that I found proof of men having been shot for desertion.

I had been asked to go through the numerous boxes and company files, and to get rid of anything not required – and using my discretion, destroy or retain the papers.

It was a long and very tedious job to do conscientiously, and when I eventually came across 'Crime Books' sitting alone in the hut, candle lit, with boxes, papers, books, maps, etc, going back over the four years, I thought, 'Did we ever really have men tied to the gun-wheel?'

Men were tied to the wagon or gun-wheels for hours as part of punishment for refusing to obey an order – and I thought I might find confirmation. It was getting late, I was tired, and the candles were flickering as though they too were fed up. Flip, flip – over went the pages as I scanned them. 'Seven days for this', 'Fourteen days Confined to Barracks for that.' Twenty days, etc – and then the shock. It was like seeing a ghost, there written and printed in indelible pencil on the Army graph-squared paper was the record of a man shot for desertion – one of my own battalion. I'm sure that my hair must have stood up – I was so shocked. There was the official report and finding of a Field General Court Martial of a young soldier found guilty of desertion and shot on Kemmil Hill by British soldiers, where only less than a year before we had all been fighting the Boche.

Perhaps it would not have been stamped in my memory had I not been there, over the same ground, and I thought of the grey days, mist, gas, shelling, the killed and screaming wounded, as I slowly tore out the page. What prompted me to do so, or whether or not I intended to destroy it later so that nobody should know that we had had a man shot for cowardice, I don't know. I was dazed and felt so sorry that had he had the strength to hold out, now that it was all over, he would have been with us – but of course with the heavy casualty lists at that time, he might have been killed anyway – but this, by your own men, was what shook me.

How was his death reported? 'Killed in action'? Did his people know that when he was brought back to France, it was to be shot for cowardice? Surely not, and it is so hard to be a hero and so easy to be a coward and there is so little difference in what prompts a man to run forward and kill Germans or in sheer desperation, through the torture of months in the line, run away.

Even generals broke under the strain and were sent home, but they did not shoot them. More likely they were pensioned off, but when it was a case of a private soldier it was indeed a fact that they were sometimes shot as a horrible example to the others. 'Behave yourselves, or this is what will happen to you.'

I read those cold words, 'Plea – Not Guilty. Finding of the Court – Guilty. Sentence – to suffer death by being shot.' Were there other cases in the 'Crime Book'? I would never know, for I folded the page up and put it in my tunic pocket. Tearing up the book I fed it into the stove. Nobody else saw the book or the page I had taken out, I had not any special reason for taking it unless it had been to convince myself later that I had not just dreamed it. This feeling has, in a way, been confirmed by the few people who have seen this record, including members of the police, church, etc, and to a man they have all seemed incredulous when told that hundreds of British soldiers had been shot in this way.

Captain James Lovegrove
South Lancashire Regiment

There were many cases of harsh punishments for men in the front line – a whole lot... 307 of them. They were shot for cowardice. One case was that of my father's workman, who was a trimmer in his tailor's business. He joined up in the London division. He was a very short man and the most lovable little chap – and one night they had a raid on and he was missing – so he was court martialled and he would normally have been shot. According to the evidence, when they got back from the raid he was sitting in a corner of a trench reading a book by the light of a Tommy candle – that's a little round burner with methylated spirit which you used to heat up a mug of something hot. The prosecutor asked what was the book, and he told them it was Bram Stoker's *Dracula* – and they let him off! It was quite remarkable – there was a battle on and he never heard anything – he was engrossed reading this book. That was a funny case – they didn't prove that he had escaped from his post; he just never went over the top. How would you know that you had to go over the top if somebody didn't tell you?

Often no account was taken of the men's mental state. At the beginning of the war it was different. When I went to Felixstowe first there were twin brothers – one was the adjutant, one was the company commander, and they went straight to France with the draft. They both ended up back here in England with shell-shock. That was from 1914, and when we got back from the Front in 1919 they were still home and wearing their Mons medal.

As the war progressed the problem of shellshock was increasingly side-lined. I saw some dreadful cases. I had two men who, depending on which way the wind was blowing, had to march either at the front or the back of the platoon because they were incontinent all the time. I couldn't get them back to England.

I had been in hospital with an injury and I learned that these two men had been sent up to HQ, and had been reprimanded. I was complaining that I never knew they had been sent – but that somebody must have known. My sergeant said, 'Of course we got rid of them – gave Division a sample of what it's like.' Certainly, the pair of them were absolutely mental – they couldn't have fired a rifle, if they got one. I thought nobody could possibly put them in the Front Line – but there they were, up at Ypres and they were incontinent all the time.

Gertrude Farr

Widow of Private Harry Farr, 1st Battalion West Yorkshire Regiment,
executed for cowardice

I didn't get to hear what Harry was going through – you had to use your judgment from the people who came back. They sent me a letter from the War Office. 'Dear Madam, we regret to inform you that your husband has died. He was sentenced for cowardice and was shot at dawn on the 16th October.' That was all I got, through the post. I got hold of that letter and I pushed it right down in my blouse in case anybody saw it – and nobody knew – even my mother didn't know.

Nobody could say anything to help me – my sisters were cross with me because I'd kept it to myself for six months. I managed to pay for my accommodation until six months had passed. I was supposed to go on the pension – but I didn't. When I went to the Post Office, the six months had expired, and the lovely lady, who had known me since a little girl, said, 'I'm sorry Mrs Farr; there isn't any money for you this week. You really should be on your pension now. The allowance has been stopped and you're now a war widow, with a war widow's pension.' I kept looking for the pension, but still there was no money. But in the meantime, I got a letter from the War Office, saying 'Owing to the death of your husband – owing to the way he died – you and your daughter are not eligible for the pension.' That's all I got. I had no income at all – I was left stranded and penniless. I had to go to the soldiers' and sailors' orphanage for help – the Post Office lady told me I ought to ask if I could get relief there. In the meantime, my little bit of rent was going up and up, and when my landlady knew I wasn't getting a pension, she told me she wanted her room back – I'd got to get out of the house. A friend took me in and put me and Gertie up in one of her rooms until we found another place.

Armistice Day – don't mention it! I can't describe the feelings.

I feel absolutely dreadful and every year I feel worse. Every year I see all those men who came back – the veterans – and my husband should have been there among them. It's very distressing when I see them all.

CHAPTER 6

Returning to Work

Men who had left civilian jobs to join up were assured of their posts still being open when they returned – but the employment climate at home had changed. Many businesses not engaged in war-related work had gone to the wall during the conflict, and now the fighting had stopped, munitions and other related industries were closed down and their workers laid off.

Women who had stepped in to fill the absent men's jobs – and had become accustomed to doing a day's work for a welcome wage – were now dismissed. But even the men who resumed their old jobs were not safe. The production industry was in decline and the economy at a low ebb, and soon companies across the country were laying off staff or going out of business altogether.

Some men waited for years before getting work – others took up any opportunity to get more education or retrain. But for the returning servicemen, Lloyd George's 'Land Fit for Heroes' was a grave disappointment, and by 1921, when Armistice Day was observed, there were demonstrations by out-of-work veterans, carrying placards – 'The dead are remembered, but we are forgotten'.

Lieutenant James Lovegrove
South Lancashire Regiment

The experience of the war altered me completely. I have two photographs of me with only a year's difference between them. One was taken just before I went out to France and one when I came back, taken by the same photographer in Felixstowe. In the second, I'm practically dead – I can't believe that photograph.

When I got back, instead of returning to my friends, I and some others were transferred to the camp at Aldershot. There were seventy of us in the mess, all raring to get back our youth, but we had to keep marching up and down outside the mess while the band played. Then at the officers' mess bugle call, we'd go inside where the colonel would come in with the second-in-command and the adjutant and we all had to stand to attention.

My money at the time was ten shillings a day and out of that I had to pay the mess bill. It was five bob for port – which I didn't even drink – and I didn't see why I should do this. I was with six other men and I said, 'The colonel tells us the same old tales, and he sits with all his toadies around him, laughing at the same old stories until twelve o'clock at night, drinking and having a good time – and we have to sit at the table.' I thought the major was my friend.

So I went in one night to see him and told him what was the matter. I said, 'I haven't had any youth. I have had no decent upbringing but war, and when I came back, I found that both the partners of the firm where I was learning architecture were dead and the firm has closed down, so now I have got to start again. I have no articles.' He said, 'What is all this leading up to?' I said, 'Please, in the evening, when the King's health is drunk and we're allowed to smoke, couldn't you allow that any officer who would wish to leave the mess may do so?' 'And how many of you feel like that?' I said, 'There are seven of us.' He said. 'I see – and are you in charge?' I said, 'Yes.' House arrest! He sent me up before the colonel for mutiny. I went back to the others and I said, 'I can't believe it! They have been home here, all this time, living on the fat of the land – everybody seems to be on rationing except them. They are having port and cigars and all this good living, with the band playing.' In the end I didn't have to go before the colonel. I got a message to say that we would hear something in the mess that evening.

They decided that any officer would be allowed to leave once permission had been given to smoke. We were sitting around a separate table, and after we had the loyal toast, I got up straight away – but none of the others moved. I thought, 'you dirty dogs' and I walked out. So I ended up before the colonel, so I explained myself. He said, 'Why do you want to leave the army?' I said, 'Because you won't let me get married.' He replied, 'Of course not. You haven't got any private income. You have to have a private income to be able to live.' I told him I didn't care, and that I couldn't stand being alone any longer. He said, 'What do you mean?' I repeated that I wanted to get married. He said, 'But you are not even twenty-one yet boy. Does your father know? I said, 'No I haven't told him.' I explained that I had a girl, and wanted to marry her – but that there was someone else after her – another officer. 'Don't you realise that it's worse for the married men, they know what it is like being separated – the unmarried ones don't know what they're missing. Anyway, we are moving to Borden camp tomorrow, I won't put your name on the list, if you would like to go and discharge yourself you can.' And that is what I did.

Sergeant Harold Flood
Royal Field Artillery

I was called to the CO in Siegburg and he gave me the surprise of my life. 'Flood, I have received an order from above to recommend a man for the new course to be started for the training personnel for the new Army Educational Corps. Would you like to accept?'

I couldn't get my 'Yes sir!' out quickly enough. I was dispatched to Newmarket, where the Education Course was being held. I found myself among a group of men, some of whom were teachers before the war. Our three tutors introduced us to the new ideas set out by the Government and the Ministry of War.

I completed the course and left with a First Class Certificate as an Educational Instructor with the AEC, starting with the rank of sergeant. I had joined the army and been granted my request to be in the Royal Field Artillery, and was posted as a recruit to Fulwood Barracks, Preston. Now I was posted back to Fulwood Barracks as assistant teacher under the schoolmaster, Mr Gearing. What a lovely change!

I was enjoying life and my new work. It really was a happy time, doing work which was appealing to me and satisfying – and it was my introduction to the job of teaching children, of which I had had no experience beyond that of pre-war Sunday school teaching.

However, soon I was told I'd been selected from the North Western Command to be Schoolmaster-in-Charge of the King's Shropshire Light Infantry stationed at Copthorne Barracks, Shrewsbury. Mr Gearing ended the interview saying, 'I am sorry to lose you, but I do congratulate you. You are now really set on a good course. One day you will find yourself enjoying life on the lovely station of Gibraltar, and having holidays in North Africa, ending your days as a colonel.'

Gunner William Towers
Royal Field Artillery

I qualified after my tailoring course – I passed the exam and they gave me a £10 cheque and a kit of tools for qualifying, and that was it. When I went for a job, the fellow laughed at me. He said, 'Hand tailoring is out of date. It is all going to be machine work now.' I thought, 'My God, I've been stumped again! Qualified in another trade – and it's out of date.' So I couldn't get a job.

Next day I went to find Mr Gaunt at the shop and he invited me to come in and sit down. We went through all the formalities, but then we started talking about other things. He asked what I did – and I told them I was a university-trained engineer. The company made the castings for metalwork, and he asked me if I could do that sort of work. I told him I'd made the original of the mould that they showed me. Nothing happened for a while – I hadn't had my leg fitted at that stage – but once I had it, they sent for me and offered me a job. I would have taken anything at the time, but they offered me this job and the manager of the works, who was an engineer, said he'd teach me everything for that particular job.

I thought this was lovely – but I had to go five or six miles to work every morning taking two trams and walking a lot. I had to be there for eight o'clock, so it was pretty hard work. I left and went straight to another similar outfit in Kirkstall. I think he resented me going. At the next place they were just as difficult as at Bramley. They resented me being there because I wasn't a Kirkstall man – I was a foreigner. They didn't like me and they played all sorts of tricks – did anything they could to upset me. Me having a false leg didn't enter into it. They had never stepped out of bed, so to speak. The war had been a boom-time to them and they were sorry when it was over.

Corporal Joseph Yarwood
94th Field Ambulance, RAMC

In April we eventually came back via Dunkirk then, being a Yorkshire division, we went up to Richmond. There we handed in all our kit and we were put on a train at York. There were four of us, and we decided we'd have a few days together before we went our separate ways. We went to Knaresborough and found a little pub doing bed and breakfast, and we booked in for our final fling. Half way through this little break we started to get short of money. When we got our demob suits we were allowed to keep our greatcoats, but if you handed it in they'd give you £2 for it – so we all handed in our greatcoats, got the two pounds each, so we could afford to stay a few more days together.

After that I needed to get a job. There was my old firm, but I didn't bother with them after they let me know I needn't hurry to get back. I thought, 'To hell with them. Whatever happens I am not going back there.'

Before the war I'd been very keen on getting a good education, and now I discovered that there were grants available to soldiers who had come out of the army, to help them get a better education. I applied in writing – but they never had the courtesy to reply. I wrote them a rude letter to say that I'd served my country for three and a half years – and was angry that they couldn't even bother to reply to my letter. That brought forth a reply from someone very high up in the education department. I went to see him and put my case to him. He said, 'I quite understand what you say, but my advice to you is to go and complete your matriculation, then you can come straight to us and we'll give you a grant.'

Carrying on my studies to matriculate was going to prove expensive – and I was on the dole at 29 bob a week. Out of that I had to give my mum a pound a week towards my keep, so I hadn't got a lot of money. I did get a 'bounty' of £25 when I came out of the army, but I spent £20 of that having a good suit made, because if I wanted to get a job I'd need to be respectably dressed. For several weeks I went to Westminster Polytechnic, two or three times a week. They set me essays and homework – then suddenly I got a job with a firm in Shaftesbury Avenue. The job was working for a French bloke who ran a business with automatic slot-machine – he had these machines installed all over the place. He had created a map of the battle areas of France, and if you touched the different towns with a special pointer it would light up the areas where there was fighting in each year of the war.

He took me on to help make these maps and then go out on the road and flog 'em. He engaged a lot of girls to assemble the maps, and I was put in charge. I used to work late evenings, Saturdays and Sundays without a penny overtime – and of course that put paid to my further education. But when I went back after Christmas, the job had folded.

I wasn't so much bitter about being on the dole as frustrated because I'd wasted three or four years – a very important time of my life – when I should have been making some headway. Now, at that critical time of my life I was having to make a fresh start.

Maybe it was a bit cheeky, but I wrote to an ex-officers association. I went to see them and they gave me a job. They knew about my background – that I'd been on the road for a hardware firm before the war broke out – so they got me a job with a branch of Joe Lyons – the catering people – who had bought the firm. They made automatic routers for making wood mouldings, picture frames and rails. The Lyons group were interested because they were always opening new shops and they decorated these with a lot of elaborate mouldings. My job was to work there as a mechanic. I was there for four or five months, and picked up some experience of sheet metal work and I used to make lengths of galvanized tubing to suck the sawdust from the machine. I also used to make covers for the machines and do tool-making.

I used to get a labourer's money, which saved them the cost of a mechanic – which would have been twice as much as I was getting – but I was glad to do it. I always liked working with my hands and I thought I had a good job there. But then what happened? There was a coal strike in 1921, and we were all laid off. They said they would write to me when they were taking people on again. But I never heard from them. I understand that most of the fellows went back but I never did – so bang went the moulding job.

Private Thomas Hooker

Machine Gun Corps

The Army was an experience – you got to know people, and we were all boys together. We all thought that was the end – the war to end all wars – that everybody had learnt that lesson. I suppose the people who studied those things thought otherwise, but ordinary people never thought there would be another one.

We came back to a worldwide depression and unemployment – we were glad to get a job, and I went back as a student at the London School of Economics. As a bit of strategy on the part of the government they gave us £200 – and were told to find ourselves a school. I had matriculated at St Dunstan's and I was able to join the London School of Economics, which was a small affair in those days – less than three thousand students.

I stayed at the LSE until I realized it was getting me nowhere, so I took a job in the Civil Service for six months – but I couldn't stand that either. I went back to the company that I'd served for about six months pre-war and they simply said, 'There's no job for you – we've got our other men back.' There was a real post-war depression – everybody was out of luck, with strikes galore, culminating in the general strike of 1926 – so we had no time to worry about the 'land fit for heroes'. We didn't consider ourselves heroes anyway.

Private George Grunwell

16th Battalion, West Yorkshire Regiment

I, along with other men, started to look for work – but it was fruitless. I went back to Bradford, and I was out of work there for three years. I tried everything and anything – postal work – a course in motoring. But it was all fruitless – there were too many people, and drivers were ten a penny. We were queuing up at the labour exchange, but there were no jobs there for us – all they could do was hand out unemployment pay, which was eighteen shillings a week.

I was back and living at home, but drawing unemployment pay went down very badly with me. I suppose I didn't feel so badly about there being no jobs – I'd got away from the war, so even if life wasn't good, it was far better than the mud fields of Flanders. We were all in similar circumstances, so we just carried on.

At that time there was a government scheme, whereby they would allow a certain sum of money to any employer who took on an ex-serviceman for training. Eventually I sat down at a tailor's board and started learning the trade. In the summertime there was plenty of tailoring work, although in the winter it was a bit patchy. I stayed because there was no prospect of anything else. I learned to make clothes and just carried on. Eventually I got married and brought up a family and it was a case of sticking to one's trade. It was all right until the Second World War began, and with that work fell off dramatically. I managed to get a job in a wool warehouse – it was just labouring work – and that was where I was until I retired.

I hadn't given any deep thought to my future when I joined the army. For me it was a case of joining up to get away from the drab life of being on one's own in a little brick building and just serving men as they left with their loads of stuff for the mills and the gasworks. Life in the army promised more variety – more going on. After the war was over it gave me pause to look back and consider all the lives that had been sacrificed. It made me feel that, if there was such a thing, and if I was to be called up to serve in another war, I would certainly take a stand as a Christian man and come out dead against any service where men are compelled to fight.

I never became an active pacifist after the war – besides, I was middle aged by the next war so I wasn't approached to fight again.

Private Joseph Pickard
1/5th Battalion, Northumberland Fusiliers

I had the twelve months of out-patient treatment – which brought me to May 1922. All the time I was wondering what the devil I could do. I was determined I wasn't going to be like some of them who walked the streets with a stick, trying to live on a pension. So I found out that the government had what they call an instructional factory at Birtley, in Durham. There was a whole list of things you could train for – tailoring, cobbling – but I didn't fancy that either. I had worked on a lathe before and used my hands earlier on. However, I thought if I went in for watch-making I could work sitting down. I couldn't stand at the bench to work – that was my trouble. I got invited up to Newcastle and I had to go in front of a board of the Watchmakers' Guild who had shops up in Newcastle. They asked me why I wanted to work in watch-making, and to see if my hands were suitable. After one thing and another, I got invited to start at Birtley. There were instructors there who acted as supervisors, and there were three different shops. You started like an apprentice – you were given a file and a square and a block of oak and you had to square that piece of oak. That was the start.

The whole set-up was run by the government for ex-soldiers – but not specifically for wounded veterans. It was for anybody who had been in the forces. I stayed there for around sixteen months, towards the end of which we were invited to go out and find a job on Civvy Street. If you found a job you'd be set up with a kit of tools.

So I came back to Alnwick – you naturally go back to where you belong, even though there weren't that many people who knew me by then. The government would pay a certain amount towards my wage, so I went to a shop where I knew the owner, and he agreed to take me on for at least six months. This meant that I could collect a kit of tools – I had signed for them and they were all mine! At the end of six months this man asked me if I wanted to stay on. I said I would like to, and he took me on for another six months. I went on serving my apprenticeship, and my wage gradually went up. At the end of the period of apprenticeship, he asked again if I wanted to stay – and I said I'd like to.

That was September 1923. By the beginning of the last war I was running that shop, doing the jobs on the bench, organizing the office work, doing estimates and all aspects of the business. I was there thirty odd years.

Lance Corporal William Cowley
Army Service Corps

Eventually I demobbed myself. I was in charge – all our officers had gone and left me in charge, with a corporal in command of the whole lot, and I thought, 'I am going to be here forever.' My wife said I was the last one to come home. I was responsible for everything, so I got the forms, signed them myself and came home, leaving the lads with the corporal in charge. It didn't matter to me – I was out of it. I thought, 'I am going to have a man's furlough', so I went to my old firm and saw the boss – he was pleased to see me back and asked when I could start. I said I wanted a month's holiday first, so eventually I started back at the same firm as before the war – at a very low wage. Admittedly it was a lot more than before the war, but it was still very low. I'd expected better treatment.

Private Basil Farrer
Army Pay Corps

At the time I was rather pleased to be demobbed, but I don't know why. I might have done better had I stayed in. I would have eventually risen in rank and would have got commissioned. However, I wouldn't have lived the life that I did, and I doubt whether, unless I was extremely lucky, I would have been quite as comfortable as I am now. I went back to Nottingham and went to the pay office with a view to being taken on as a civilian clerk. I arrived at the pay office in civvies and the sergeant major spotted me and asked what I was doing out of uniform. He knew I was a regular soldier because they were demobilizing as well as discharging. I was discharged as unfit for further service, because I'd got a contract for twelve years with the army – seven years with the colours and five on reserve. I had only done six, so he knew that I wouldn't have been demobilized. I said, 'Sergeant Major, I have not been demobilized – I have been discharged,' and I quoted the relevant paragraph. The upshot was that I started back as a civilian clerk.

Private Ernie Rhodes
16th Battalion, Manchester Regiment

When I came back from the war, the Eccles Industrial Society got me out of the army and gave me my old job back. But that only lasted four years. A big combine bought them out and I found myself on the dole. The Ford Motor Company used to be at Trafford Park and then they moved to Dagenham. I knew two lads who worked there, and I asked them if there was any chance of some work. They didn't say 'no', so I asked my dad for £10 to go down to Dagenham for the chance of getting some work there.

I got the train to Charing Cross, then on to Dagenham. Before I went in I'd been talking to a chap who'd been at Austin motors, and he had come to Dagenham to better himself. When I got a chance to speak to someone, I told them how I had been in cotton trade. They said there was nothing they could offer me. The chap I'd spoken to earlier asked how I'd got on and I said, 'No chance'.

He said, 'I bet there is some job they can give you. Come back in the morning, and if you manage to get in again, tell them you used to be a fitter and that you have done a lot of turning.' So I did – I went back the following morning with my good suit on – and I got a job! When I went back next day to start work, this supervisor took me to a machine and talked a lot of technical jargon – and ended up telling me to be careful. I'd got no idea what he was talking about, but I daren't tell him because I'd be kicked out. But I managed, and eventually got pretty good at the job.

Trooper Sydney Chaplin
1st Battalion, The Northamptonshire Yeomanry

In 1916 I went into the nearby town with a limber and two horses and I saw an officer sitting very uncomfortably on a horse. The animal was throwing its head up, and dancing around. The officer called to me and said, 'Do you think there's something wrong? This horse is usually very quiet to ride.' I told him to dismount and straight away I found that the bit had been pulled up tight in the horse's mouth and the curb chain was also too tight. So I slacked the curb and dropped the bit and soon the horse was quite docile. He thanked me and we had a talk. Then he said, 'I would like to be able to have a drink with you, but that's against orders.' So he handed me a ten-franc note and said, 'Drink my health,' and we shook hands.

In 1923, I was still without regular work – just odd jobs when I could get them – when I was told that the Corps of Commissionaires were interviewing ex-servicemen in London. So I managed to scrape together enough to pay for a return ticket to London and to cover expenses. I was interviewed by a major who took my particulars, checked my discharge papers, then informed me that, owing to the number of applications, it would be a very long while before they could offer me a post. So that was it.

I had a walk round and eventually sat down on a seat on the Embankment. I must have dozed off, because it was dark when I woke up, so I decided to stay put until the morning. I woke as the dawn was breaking, and what a sight it was. All the seats were full of old soldiers in all sorts of dress – mostly khaki – and a lot more were lying on the steps, some wrapped up in old newspapers. Men who had fought in the trenches, now unwanted and left to starve, were all huddled together. I was on the end of a seat, so I eased my fingers into my pocket to get a cigarette, as I didn't want to wake the chap who was leaning against me, then I managed to light up. 'That smells good,' said the voice of the man I thought was asleep. I recognized him at once. I handed him a cigarette and said, 'Would you like a light, Major?' 'Good Lord! You, Corporal!' We stood up and looked at each other. 'Well, what about a spot of tea?' I said. He just spread out his hands and said, 'I am flat broke.' So I took him to a coffee stall and we had a mug of tea and two slices of bread and dripping each. The Major told me he had been caught out by one of the many crooks who were battening on old soldiers. They offered shares in a business, producing false books, and when the money had been paid over, they just disappeared. All his money had gone, however, he was going to see one of his old junior officers that day, and he was hoping to get a break. After an argument, I persuaded him to accept a few cigarettes and a shilling to tide him over.

I spent the day looking for work, but there were no vacancies anywhere. Finally I went into a cinema for a rest in the three-penny seats. It was dark when I came out and headed for St Pancras Station for the night train. As I was passing a shop doorway, I heard someone crying. I stopped and looked in and saw a man wearing an army greatcoat with a turban on his head and a tray suspended from his neck with lucky charms on it. Another man, unwanted after three years in the trenches. He and his wife were penniless, but some crook offered him a chance to earn easy money if he could find five shillings. His wife pawned her wedding ring to get it, and in return he got a tray, a turban and a dozen or so lucky charms to sell at sixpence each. What a hope! Now after a day without anything to eat or drink, he was broken-hearted at the thought of going home to his wife without a penny. He was an ex-Company Sergeant-Major. I sorted my cash out (one shilling and tenpence), gave him the shilling and a fag. Then I carried on to the station, spent my remaining tenpence at the coffee stall and got the train home.

Lieutenant James Lovegrove
South Lancashire Regiment

They'd started up an officers' employment bureau at Horrock's Hotel in The Strand, so I went along and was shown up to a room where a colonel was conducting interviews and a young chap at the table filled in the forms. The colonel asked me what I had in mind, so I said, 'I have an uncle in California and I would like to go fruit farming there, but I need a little bit of tuition before I go there.' He asked, 'How much money has your uncle got?' I said, 'It's nothing to do with money. With all due respect, you are supposed to find us a job.' At this point he went out of a room, and this young fellow said to me, 'You'll never get anywhere with the attitude you're taking. You slip him a fiver and you will get your job all right.' I went downstairs and I saw these other chaps and told them that it was a bit of a frame-up. Another chap and I checked up and it turned out that there were chaps being sent up to Newcastle to get a job in shipping, but the shipyard was closing down, and they'd never heard of the Horrock's Hotel outfit. We thought they must have made a mistake, so this chap went down to Southampton shipyard – and they were closing down too. And so it went on, at every place they were sending people for work. It was a scandal and it was closed down. Those colonels must have been on army pensions and they were getting extra money for doing this. Nothing was said about it.

Another scandal was about medals. At one time, an NCO came along offering medals to the men at so much each. So much for an MC and so on. They'd got them to spare, because if you won a big battle, the whole division was awarded medals. As an officer, I used to recommend the bravest man – I was given the option to choose a recipient. They practically served the medals up with the rations – any medal bar the Victoria Cross. Somebody else got the medal that was due to me. My experiences made me grow up terribly quickly. I learnt that there are a lot of toadies about – not genuine people.

Private Francis Sumpter
17th Field Ambulance, RAMC

The Westminster Academy of Fashion, Oxford Street, was running a three-month course for £20 – but where was I going to get £20? Eventually my father-in-law lent me the money and I took a course, learning how to cut patterns – and at the end I got the diploma. When I finished, the head of the academy suggested I open a shop. I was given a grant of £80 and I was told I would get the money within a month. During that time I looked around and found a shop in Upper Street, Islington and I paid the first week's rent on it. Then I got a letter from the grants people saying they were very sorry, but as I was not a conscript but a freely enlisted soldier, I was not entitled to a grant. Apparently only conscripted men were eligible for a grant. I was disgusted, because I had gone away to war, leaving a happy home with my three brothers and a family. I had gone all through the war and I had learned my trade. I had been a skilled man and had a good future in front of me with a good wage in the bespoke handmade shoe and boot trade – and now here I was, unable to go back to my job. What's more, my two brothers were killed, and my father's workshop had been turned over to military work, so his few staff became redundant. He died during the war and my mother had become mentally ill after losing her two boys. The war messed up our whole home and family. I had survived throughout the war – and now at the end of it, I had nothing. Even the grant had been taken away from me.

I had to take work wherever I could find it. First I applied to be a tram driver/conductor and the LCC put me through a little gymnastic course and found the weakness in my left arm, so they turned me down. That was the first of a number of jobs I failed to get because of that arm. Eventually I got a job as storekeeper at a tobacco factory in Shoreditch where they used to make shag. One day some stuff came into the store and it had to be kept on a high shelf because if it was stored low, it would deteriorate. I got a ladder to get up to a shelf and I asked somebody else to hand me up the stuff so I could put it up with my good hand. The foreman said 'What's wrong with your left arm?' I explained that I couldn't use it as I'd been wounded, and in my pay packet that weekend I was given a week's notice because I wasn't fit for the job.

Then I got a job as a postman and I was sent to a Post Office as a sorter. I found I could sort letters as quick as the next man. Then I was put on a loading detail where you had to throw the bags into a van from the bank – and I couldn't do that. If I threw a bag with my left arm it went anywhere except where I wanted it to go, so I would lift on the right side and carry the bags rather than throwing them. The rest of the squad got difficult about it. 'Get a move on! We want to get finished!' The sooner you packed up the sooner you got home, and I slowed them down – so after two or three years of this I was ostracized, and the boys went to the trade union to get rid of me. The trade unions tried to get rid of me, but the Assistant Inspector wouldn't listen to them. He said, 'You've no complaint. We can't get rid of him – and he can do the job. I know you boys want to get home early, but the time allowance is ample. You boys have plenty of time for loading, so your complaint isn't justified.' That only made the men worse. I stuck the job for about six years, but I got fed up with it and packed it in.

Private Basil Farrer
Army Pay Corps

There was never any problem accepting the fact that women were doing the jobs usually taken by men. They were mostly young girls, and there was no friction at all. They did the jobs as well as we would.

In Oldham women drove buses, and worked in munitions factories during the war. By the time I got demobbed it was an accepted thing, because there were no men to do the job except for the very elderly or those who'd been rejected as not suitable for service – and you had to be pretty bad not to be accepted by the army! You'd be taken into some corps or other if you couldn't be on active service. The emancipation of women and their entry into all areas of work, dates from that period.

Some men who had jobs before the war came back to find their place had been taken by a woman. They might have felt that women should go back to looking after their homes, but I, as a young chap, had no opinion. The older men might have had reservations but I'd been so young when I joined the army that I didn't think about it.

When the war finished I remember one man, who was a civilian acting paymaster. It astonished us returning soldiers and caused us some resentment, that he turned up in a captain's uniform one day, and started acting very officiously. He was probably an accountant or a bank clerk in civil life – but had been made a captain. We certainly resented the fact that he was civvy one day and captain the next. We had to salute him and address him as 'Sir'!

Norah Beale
Clerical worker

For years I worked mornings doing some book-keeping at the National Deposit Friendly Society. Then, during the war I got to do office work because all the fellows were away.

I used to go to evening classes, for shorthand, typing, cookery and sewing. My mother thought it was good for young girls to go to the evening classes. I had to pay for the classes – I think it was about half a crown for the term.

Occasionally I used to go to a social – and church on Sunday, and the odd visit to the cinema. I didn't meet my husband until 1926. He was out of work for a long time, until 1927 or 28. The unemployment was terrible, and we couldn't get married because he didn't have a job.

Eva Marsh
Women's Land Army

I loved the life – the fresh air and being all on my own – it was lovely. I was sorry when I had to give it up. As usual, it was always me they called on if there was any emergency at home and my granny had fallen and broken her hip and was paralysed – so I had to go home to look after her. There was nobody else to do it, so I had to leave my lovely land army.

We got paid seven shillings a week and it was all-in – everything was paid for. Seven shillings clear seemed like a lot of money to me, especially as I got nothing when I was working at home – no pocket money. My father told my mother that she should pay me the same as I was getting in the Land Army, but she never did. Then granny died and I decided to go out and get a job. Dad said, 'But you've got money!' and I said, 'I've never had a penny.' Of course, that made trouble between my mum and dad, but anyway I got a job looking after a little boy – oh, he was lovely! He was only two years old and he was my boy. As for pay for looking after him, I took what they could give. I was living in, so I had a roof over my head. I earned about £3 a month, and I was happier than I'd ever been before.

By the time I got married, I was forty-five! I said I would never marry, because the boy I was engaged to never came back from the war. I didn't want anyone else, but then my husband came along.

Annie May Martin
Women's Army Auxiliary Corps

I don't think the war changed me – I did the work I was accustomed to doing. The living conditions were different, but one soon returned to normal. It seemed one had hardly been away. When I got back to my office, I took my place next to a friend – I'd been away over two years and she looked at me and said, 'Have you been on holiday?' That just shows how little difference it made. You just picked up where you left off.

Captain John Grover
1st Battalion, King's Shropshire Light Infantry

After the war we all rather expected that the general atmosphere would go back to how it was pre 1914 – and for the privileged classes it was a very pleasant life. I don't think it was too unpleasant for the chaps in the villages – but none of us envisaged the development of aircraft or the motor car, which was very much in its infancy at the beginning of the war – or the experience of a world at arms. Chaps who had lived in small towns and villages were shot into a world quite different from what they knew, and it was different for them coming back. It started quite a social change, and inevitably there was bitterness, because unemployment was very bad.

Corporal Joseph Yarwood
94th Field Ambulance, RAMC

Back in England I was out of work and I had to start all over again. I was drifting around, trying to get a fresh start, when I met a couple of fellows who were university students living in Battersea. I got pally with them, and subsequently met their cousin who, like me, was involved in dramatics. She asked me to give her some help for a concert she was organizing so we started working together and got pretty thick. As a result of that, her father came to me one day and said he'd got a job for me. He had a firm working on ex-army stuff such as propellers, which you could get fairly cheap in those days – they'd cut off the blades and use the centre to make clock cases.

Sadly, that job didn't last and I found myself out of work again. A friend's father came up with a job for me. He knew a fellow who was working on the *Daily Mail*, where someone had this brainwave. In those days the cinema was something of a novelty, and they thought it would be good publicity if they made a film about the production of the *Daily Mail* to be shown in a mobile cinema touring the country. They bought a massive hangar and an ex-army lorry – which you could get cheap in those days – they had a generator fitted so it had its own electricity. I'd been trained in putting up bell tents and marquees for use as operating theatres for the field hospitals, so I was offered the job of caretaker, looking after the equipment and putting up the marquee. It was a long tent – thirty or forty yards long – made to accommodate a big audience. There was a lot of work involved – it was a canvas structure, and instead of poles it had proper framework. There was also a lining, with wooden shutters to keep the light out. It was quite an elaborate affair which had to be set up before each show. For this I was paid £4 10s a week, with two guineas a week expenses. In those days that was really good money and I was walking on air! Oh boy – I felt like a millionaire.

The film was called 'From Forest to Breakfast Table', and it started off showing how the trees were felled in Canada, from which they got the wood pulp. Then the action moved to England and they showed the various stages of production and the machines involved in producing a newspaper as the finished article, coming off the presses.

It was a popular entertainment – it was nice for people to pop in and watch it, as it only lasted twenty minutes or so.

This job started in July and it finished around the end of September when the nights were beginning to draw in. By that time it was getting too cold for people to stand out in the open so we packed it in. After that I was on the dole throughout the winter. I kept looking for work, but I wasn't trying that hard, because I'd really fallen in love with this *Daily Mail* job and I was hoping eventually that I might wangle a regular post with them – which I did.

This job for the *Daily Mail* went on for some years – but then another very interesting job turned up – sandcastles! We would start at Westcliffe on the east coast and work our way up to Hunstanton and back, then another year we would start in Westcliffe and go south along the coast to Devon and back again. This was our chief holiday, but we were working! We used to arrange sandcastle competitions for the kids. We'd get accommodation on the coast in whatever county we were in, then we'd go to the local authorities and say we wanted to hold a sandcastle competition. We asked if we could have the use of a beach at a particular time. They would give us permission and we would organize a sandcastle contest. For a morning show we'd get there about nine, cordon off a big area of sand with ropes, then we'd get the deckchair attendants to put the deckchairs all around. We'd mark out the area in squares for each competitor. Each kid entering the competition got a tin of toffee, irrespective of whether they won a prize. Essentially what they had to do was make a design in sand, but part of the publicity was that they had to build the *Daily Mail* into the design. About three-quarters of the way through the morning we would ask for several parents to come along and act as judges, and they would pick out the winners. There might be £5 for first prize and a couple of quid for a second place. Then we would move off in the afternoon to the next place.

Mrs B Brooke
Civilian returned from work escorting the bereaved to the cemeteries and battlefields in France

Altogether I had five years, from 1915, to almost the end of 1920 working in France. I came back to find my father had become ill, and we were determined that he shouldn't have to go to hospital, so we nursed him at home. He was ill for seven months, and died in 1921.

My experience of those five years stood me in very good stead when it came to settling back in the uncertain times of post-war England. I'd lost my mother when I was born, so had been brought up by my stepmother, but I was devoted to my father, so when I got back I was only too glad to look after him.

After my father died, my stepmother decided she would like to move – although we could have stayed where we were, because my father had been looking after a big estate in Cheshire, and his boss told us we could have the house as long as we wanted it. But she wanted to go to London – which surprised me because she'd been brought up in the Welsh countryside. In 1922, off we went to London, along with her own two daughters.

A friend introduced me to a community centre at St Martin in the Fields where they were doing the same sort of things that I'd got used to at Toc H and other organizations. There were a number of people there who had been working in France and I joined them, working voluntarily a few days a week, like everybody else did.

We saw the work at St Martins as very important – it wasn't like parish work, because Canon Shepherd was so big in his ideas and he, like Studdard Kennedy, was frightfully keen, and obsessed with the idea of unemployment as being the one thing that had to be put right. All of the organizations, including Toc H, were working for the same end.

The problem was general unemployment, which included people who hadn't been in the war at all. It was the beginning of serious unemployment in London.

Even though I was only a voluntary helper, they gave me accommodation in a flat above a bank in return for me running a lunch and evening recreation club for country girls who'd come up to London to work. I was able to work voluntarily all this time, because my father had been very careful to provide for my future – even down to furniture. Everything that had belonged to my mother by way of wedding presents – even if it was a bit of furniture – was set aside for me and he gave me all my own money. He arranged that, but I also had my own investments, so I never needed anything from my stepmother. There were not many people who could afford to do voluntary work, so it was a wonderful opportunity for me.

I could never have worked in France, either, had it not been for my father – but he actively encouraged it. Some time after the Armistice, he and my stepmother came out to France to see what I was doing, and stayed in the house where I was lodging.

Nurse Rosaleen Cooper
Voluntary Aid Detachment, sister of Robert Graves

I was up at Oxford, visiting one of my three brothers – my brothers all got up to Oxford on scholarships from Charterhouse – and we were out on the river in a punt. Someone said to me, 'What are you going to do now the war's over?' I said, 'I don't know. I don't want to go back to nursing, because I'd have to go back to scrubbing lockers and all my experience will be wasted.' He said, 'Why not try medicine?' It hit me like a sledgehammer to the head – that was what I would do. I would have another career.

When I got back to England there was a mood of change. I was never politically minded, and it never concerned me – although I had no doubt it should have been granted before – but it was after the end of the war that women were eventually given the vote. The theory was that women had worked so well in the war, taking on men's jobs and stepping into the breach, not just nursing, but in engineering and factories, that they had earned the vote. After the war there was quite a different feeling among women, and I did notice that.

Anonymous 'Ex-Battery Commander'
Letter to The Times, *February 4, 1920*

During the war, all those who put on the King's uniform had a great excess of friends. We were heroes in those days. Our relations, too, even our rich relatives, took a new interest in us. On leave from the Front, we were welcome and honoured guests – especially as we gained promotion – 'My cousin, the Major'.

When at last we came home, were demobilized and doffed our uniforms, we realized how much our welcome had depended on the glamour of our clothes, with all that they implied. In mufti we were no longer heroes, we were simply 'unemployed' – an unpleasant problem.

Many businessmen think they did their part in the war at home just as much as those on active service, and that no obligation rested on them to help ex-officers. I know that many of them worked long hours, even *over*worked in their country's cause, but they got a reward in experience, in an increase of income, and in good positions. And although the strain of long hours is great, their offices did not admit poison gas, mud, and shells, with the ever-present threat of sudden death.

There is a large balance outstanding to the credit of the ex-officer. Are you going to withhold payment until it is too late?

Private Turner
Machine Gun Company

One universal question which I have never seen answered – two or three million pounds a day for the 1914–19 war, yet no monies were forthcoming to put industry on its feet on our return from that war. Many's the time I've gone to bed, after a day of tramp, tramp, looking for work, on a cup of cocoa and a pennyworth of chips between us, and I would lie puzzling why, why, after all we had gone through in the service of our country, we had to suffer such poverty. We were willing to work at anything but there was no work to be had. I only had two Christmases in work between 1919 and 1939.

Private William Gillman
2/2nd Battalion, London Regiment (Royal Fusiliers)

When the time came for demobilization I was still enjoying the army life. I suppose I am an easy-going bloke – I have always taken everything in my stride. The war was a very valuable experience to me as it turned out – constantly having to keep an eye on self-preservation hardened me, and I was a lot older in experience than my years. I used to cope with things a lot more easily when I got home, because it couldn't have been any worse than trench life.

I didn't think there was any point in staying on as a regular – and I wanted to get home to civvy life, as we all did. It seemed that the whole of our lives had been spent in action. I was sent to Purfleet where I was demobbed and issued with my civilian suit. I came back to what turned out to be another vacuum, because I naturally thought I would get a job. However, I found that those that had taken demobilization ahead of me had snapped up all the jobs that were going, and by the time I got out there wasn't anything for me. I was out of work for eighteen months.

I tried to get into the Metropolitan Police first, and they asked me if I was single or married. I said I was single and they said I'd have to live in the section house. I said I couldn't do that as I'd got to support my mother, so I turned that down. Then I went to the City Police, because I was six foot two, and I was just the right height for them. I had a thorough examination until I got to the eye test. There was a Scottish optician examining and he exclaimed, 'My God, your eyes are terrible, man!' I'd never had any doubts about my eyesight, but I guess there was a standard you had to reach. 'You're a splendid physical specimen and I'll put it on your records, but your eyes – I am sorry I can't pass you.' So he wrote across my records in red ink 'SPLENDID SPECIMEN'. I was very fit and healthy and I was only twenty –

in the prime of life, you might say. Being of average intelligence, I was getting a bit frustrated to think that, after having gone through all that, I couldn't get a job.

I still wanted to get into the police, so I tried the Port of London Authority – the dock police. Again you had to sit a medical exam and undergo a six-week examination, learning the police drill – and at that medical examination they passed my eyesight – passed everything. To pass the test I needed to swim two lengths of the local baths. I was a good swimmer, so that was no problem, and I passed with flying colours. I joined them on a year's probation, by which time I would be established – or otherwise.

There were some clashes with my superiors that I didn't enjoy and I gave it up after nine months. When I left, it was deemed to be on grounds of 'temperamental inadaptability' – which went on my reference for any further employment.

I really came up against it – I couldn't get a job anywhere – there was nothing doing. Locally there was a job digging holes in the memorial ground in West Ham, which was then a practice field for West Ham Football Club, which of course the memorialists had suspended. I don't know what the internal arrangements were, but that was the job they gave us. They gave us jobs for the unemployed then – there was a lot of unemployment – and we were digging up holes and filling them up again for six weeks. That earned us enough stamps to claim unemployment benefit – which was pretty small, but at least you could pay your rent with and buy some grub.

We were in a very bad state. Unemployment was rife, there was severe depression and we were exhausted. In addition, there were all those men that had been on munitions work who had also been discharged, looking for work. This was the grim picture in England. It was just as bad in Germany. If you had any sense you realized that we weren't the only people who were suffering as a result of war – that was the inevitability of it. Later, when I did get a job, I joined a trade union. I didn't think politically about it at the time, but I knew there was something wrong. This was supposed to be a land fit for heroes, and instead the 'heroes' weren't given any respect at all. We were more or less an encumbrance to the authorities whose job it was to keep things moving, while all we were concerned about was getting a job. That was the only thing that mattered.

I helped to found the North West Ham branch of the British Legion on the Romford Road – where the ex-servicemen got together – and that was the only time we talked about the war. Even then, we talked mainly about our experiences and didn't discuss it from a political angle. You exchanged experiences and you were there to protect one another's interests. A lot of ex-soldiers in the Legion were unemployed – it was a place where you could get together and socialize, and it was some small compensation for not being at work – and you could commiserate with others in the same situation.

I only started taking an interest in politics because the trade union had introduced a political side. You paid a political levy and I naturally wanted to know what I was paying my money for. They said, 'You've joined the Labour Party'. By this time, the Labour Party was the thing to belong to, whether you were employed or not.

Frank Gillard

The railway company said, 'All men who volunteered to join the forces, we will give them their jobs back if they come back home afterwards.' We came back home, they gave us our jobs – and instead of trying to make up for lost time, working on the railway that they'd neglected, they decided to cut down. We were on just three or four days a week – and then after June 1921, everything was forgotten and they started sacking us left and right.

Private Kidd

When I was out of work I had to go before a means test panel. There was a very fat lady on the panel, cuddling a Pekinese in her lap. She said, 'We've all got to pull in our belts a hole or two these days.' I was fed up and told her, 'Your words belie your appearance. That bloody dog has had more to eat today than I have.' There was a lot of argument and it ended in a row. I was charged with common assault and got three months in Wormwood Scrubs.

Jonas Hart

When it was all over, you know what we got? A kick up the backside by the government. I've got no respect for those days. The unemployed soldier had a hell of time until the order came through that anybody employing an ex-serviceman could not sack him.

Private Humphrey Wilson
Machine Gun Corps

After the war the bottom seemed to fall out of everything – people seemed to be depressed with nothing to fight for. There was no great objective. Lloyd George said he was going to make a land fit for heroes to live in, and they jeered at him in the House of Commons, saying, 'What about this land fit for heroes to live in?' He said, 'Yes, but I didn't say before 1919.'

Ruby Ord
Women's Army Auxiliary Corps

Once we were back in England, everyone was occupied trying to get a job. It was very difficult if you had been a WAAC, because you weren't favourably looked on by people at home. We had done something that was outrageous for women to do. We had gone to France and left our homes – so we had quite a job getting fixed up with work when we got back. I got a job by accident, purely because my sister got married and her husband gave me work.

I think there was always terrible discontent because people thought they were fighting for something that was going to make everything better. But it doesn't – war never makes anything better, it makes everything worse – and people suddenly realized this. You have the artificial stimulation of the war, when you've been pepped up and kept going – then suddenly you are thrown back on your own resources, and you flop. I think this happened with the men – they were restless. They had led this peculiar life for four years – or more in some cases – and they couldn't settle back into an ordinary routine. They wanted to move – to expand. A lot of them went abroad, to the Empire – and a lot of our girls went too. If the men had wives and families, they didn't – I think they came back and were thankful. But the young ones couldn't settle. There didn't seem to be the peace in the home that there had been before – they were not content with the same simple enjoyment of life.

There was so much unemployment, and naturally women were the first out – and rightly, if they had husbands to maintain them. But the suffragettes were pressing them to hang on to their jobs and show their equality. Then there was all the craziness of the 1920s, with such things as tea dances and cocktail parties and all the night parties that the youngsters indulged in.

All this was probably a reaction following the war. A lot of them had saved quite a bit of money and now they could squander it, have a good time and let off all the feelings that had been suppressed during the war. But these smart young things didn't do the country any good – or themselves either. It never would be the same again, as it was before the Great War.

Trooper G Huggins
D Squadron, Queen's Own Oxfordshire Hussars

I left for home in February 1919, and the worst thing was leaving my horse behind. He was a lovely old chap. His name was Billy. We were told if anyone wished to buy their horses, to clip their initials on the horse's rump and give our names in, and we would be notified when they were being sold. It must have been three months later I got notice to say he was being sold at Tattersalls. I was back home, working on the farm, and my father gave me the money. I put it in my pocket – and it was a tidy sum – I took the saddle and bridle and went up on the train to London and got to Tattersalls near Hyde Park good and early to look for him before the sale. He found ME! As I was looking round I heard a horse give a knicker, a soft neighing, and I turned round and there he was. I said, 'Hello Billy', and walked up to him and he gave another knicker and rubbed his nose up and down my chest. That was at least three months after I'd last seen him. I gave fifty guineas for him – a lot of money then, but I'd have given more if needs be. I took him back in the guard's van in the train, saddled him up at the station and rode him home. My mother was waiting at the door to see if I'd got home. Oh, he was a beauty! We'd been right through the whole war together and all he'd got was a little bit of shrapnel on his nose once. I could go to any field he was in and call, 'Come on, Billy,' and he'd come galloping up to me. We had him for years, and he had a good life on the farm, did old Billy. He ended his days in clover.

Private Raynor Taylor
Welch Regiment

After demobilization we got back to work. Our Albert in particular used to go up to town and it says a lot for the British character following the demobilization that there wasn't a mutiny or similar revolt, because so many soldiers were coming back into civilian life who had been tied down by strict discipline for years and there was a tendency for them to let off steam. My father didn't like the type of people Albert was associating with – although they were people he had spent four years with in the army. Although he never came home drunk, I remember one night Albert must have got into a bit of a fight, because he came home with the loveliest black eye you had ever seen – it was a beauty. He walked in, our mother began to cry, and my dad looked him up and down. 'Serves thee right', he said and that was that. They didn't want to hear anything more about it.

My mother strongly advised me to spend all my disability money on buying a house. I can't think of anybody at our time of life who owned their house – they were all renting properties. She kept a tight hold on the bank-book while she searched around for a house for me. If she heard of one that would be coming on the market, she would go and look at it, and after she'd looked at a few, she dragged me along as well. I was only half interested, as I would have felt much better having a right good fling with money. However, eventually this row of houses came on sale – but they were all tenanted and they were being sold as a lot and if you were buying in one block it would be £120 a house, but if they had to be split up, it was £190. I suppose that's because it cost more to make the deeds out. My mother took me to see it and decided I should buy one of them, and we fixed up a mortgage from Co-op.

I used my money for the deposit, then every Friday I used to go and collect the rent of 7/4d from the tenants. In those days there was a shortage of houses, as none had been built for four years. You couldn't evict a sitting tenant unless you or they found alternative accommodation for them to move to. As a landlord you were responsible for all repairs, but the tenant was expected to do their own decorating. When I called I always used to ask if there was any news of them getting out – you always had your ear to the ground for anybody likely to move, then try to secure the house for the people who were currently in yours.

Eventually a house became vacant – there was a sequence of seven removals and we were the last in the chain. It was Christmas Eve and the seven people moved on that day to get in their own house. I arranged for the chap who did the carrying at the mill who had two horses and a lorry to come to where I was living, collect the furniture and take it to the new house. We went straight from work, and the first thing we did was strip the place down and get everything we could out on the pavement.

This fellow came with his lorry to where I was waiting outside with the furniture outside, and we began loading it up. It didn't take long because we hadn't got a lot of stuff. The last thing we loaded on the lorry was a big flock mattress. I got down and lay on top of the flock bed, clutching a great big clock.

In those days, trams used to run on tramlines in the main streets, and these lines were about the same gauge as cars and vans – so you could get the wheels stuck in the tracks. This driver kept to the tramlines, and we had a really smooth ride – marvellous. We got to our Jack's, loaded up the suite and went on to our new home. We pulled up at the front and there was my dad and my wife waiting – and we had lots of helpers. I remember we had a new carpet – I think it was three foot square – a new gas shade and an oil cloth on the bedroom floor. We had no stair carpet but there was an oil cloth in the kitchen. My wife stood there, telling everyone where to put things, and she had me running about like an old hen. In no time at all we were organized – and it was like a palace to us ... and it was properly mine!

When the carrier and his son had emptied the lorry, I said to the father, 'So, Jack, what do I owe you?' He said, 'See our Robert.' So I spoke to the son – who had done a lot of the humping about. 'Hey Bob, how much?' He said, 'Oh, give us a dollar.' Five shillings! I asked him if he fancied a drink. 'Has tha got a big jug?' I said I had, so he went to the pub and brought back a quart of ale in a big jug – so the only time I ever moved house in my life cost me just five shillings and a quart of beer. I have never moved since.

Major Richard Russell
Royal Field Artillery

They carried out a final operation on my arm in the autumn of '21, and that was the end of my troubles from my wounds. All this time my mother had had me searching for somewhere to live, and until I did, we had an uncomfortable existence living in all sorts of places.

One day in 1922, my mother rang me at the office and said she'd found a house. We went together to Purley to this place at the top of a hill, overlooking Croydon aerodrome. We had tea with the old lady, who said we needed to see her son, who was ill in bed. She asked if we would go up and say hello – which we did. As soon as I walked into the room, he said, 'Hello old chap! What are you doing in my house?' He had served with me! We bought that house – which cost me a lot. I got a mortgage with my mother, we moved in and we were very happy there for twenty years.

I went back to the firm I had worked for before the war. They were supposed to have made around £300,000, but one of the partners and cashier had embarked on a lot of rash financial experiments. I always felt bitter about them because I worked on commission, and when they failed they owed me £2400 – which was all the money I had in the world. In the end, I got just £600, and I was left without a job.

CHAPTER 7

Commemoration and Reflection

Considering the war – immediately after the Armistice or with the benefit of many years' hindsight – the men and women touched by the conflict bore lasting effects.

Some reflected with gratitude that they had been spared, while others, brutalized by their time in the trenches, found their personalities and temperaments irrevocably changed. Their views reflect the whole range of emotion, from sorrow to anger and guilt at surviving.

Certainly none imagined another world conflict. This had been the war to end all wars, and in its wake an industry sprang up around tours of the battlefields, selling 'souvenirs' and visiting the cemeteries. Returning over a decade later to the scene of the conflict, veterans found the devastated lands transformed – only in their heads did those images of death and destruction live on. But remembrance was paramount to convince the British public that their sacrifice had not been in vain. The Cenotaph and the 'Tomb of the Unknown Warrior' still stand as memorials to the dead.

King George V
(letter published in the *Daily Express* 19 July 1919)

To these, the sick and wounded who cannot take part in the festival of victory, I send out greetings and bid them good cheer, assuring them that the wounds and scars so honourable in themselves, inspire in the hearts of their fellow countrymen the warmest feelings of gratitude and respect.

Manchester Evening News, 10 July 1919
(on the announcement of 'Peace Day')

Sir,

I'm sure the title 'Peace Day' will send a cold shiver through the bodies of thousands of 'demobbed' men who are walking about the streets of Manchester looking for a job. Could a term be found that would be more ironical for such men? Perhaps, after the Manchester and Salford Corporations have celebrated this 'Peace' and incidentally will have wasted the thousands of pounds which it will cost, they will devote their spare time to alleviating the 'bitterness' and 'misery' which exist in the body and mind of the unemployed ex-soldier.

It is high time some very forcible and active measures were taken. Many Manchester businessmen refuse to employ the ex-soldier on the grounds that he has lost four years of experience in this line or that line of business through being in the army. What a splendid and patriotic retort to make to the men who were chiefly instrumental in saving their business from being in the possession of the Hun.

Kate Shallis
Mother who lost four sons in the war

The celebration at the Cenotaph was too wonderful to be real – so it seemed to me. Today, looking down upon it all from a high window in Whitehall, I had thoughts such as no-one has been able to express to me ... the King came and placed his wreath at the foot of the Cenotaph, while the Queen at her window facing mine stood straight and still watching him. I felt that the King and Queen and I and the masses of people were just one big family, thinking together the same dear thoughts of our million sons who died for us. I could see the Queen's face quite clearly and it seemed to me to be pale with the sorrow which she was feeling for all the mothers whose sons never came back home. I felt she was proud of my four boys who gave their lives for King and Country, and that she was sorry for me ... I felt proud of my four sons and of their courage; I felt proud that I was their mother.

The ceremony at the Cenotaph must have given, I think, some little satisfaction to all the mothers whose sons died. It must have made them feel that their boys' sacrifice and their own had not been forgotten.

The *Daily Herald*, 12 November 1920

At eight o'clock the people stood eight deep in a double line from the Cenotaph to Trafalgar Square. From here, the queue stretched down Northumberland Avenue to the Embankment and along the Embankment to Westminster. From there it doubled back to Trafalgar Square.

These were no mere sightseers, these men and women slowly moving along in that great pilgrimage, tired and drooping with the long waiting. They were the mothers and the fathers and the wives and the children of the great army of the dead.

There were old mothers in dingy black, down whose furrowed cheeks the tears trickled; there were young women who carried in their arms the little ones grown sleepy on the long trail.

And all along the way the air was heavy with the pungent earthy odour of white chrysanthemums and the strong sweetness of the lilies that so many of the pilgrims carried.

At last, through the mist, the noble lines of the Cenotaph appeared, now standing twelve feet deep in flowers. Here the policemen gently marshalled the pilgrims into double file, and with bowed heads they passed, the men with bare heads, and the women, many of them with their faces buried in their handkerchiefs.

At either end of the enclosed space more flowers were banked high. And then were piled higher and higher as woman after woman, and here and there a child, stooped to add their tribute. Many of the women, bowed and broken, were overcome with weeping as they were led away.

Gunner William Towers
Royal Field Artillery

I'd had my leg amputated over a year before, but I went to a café for dinner on Armistice Day, and was sitting at a window from where I could hear a band playing. I looked down the road, and it was my own battery coming home. As they passed the Town Hall, the Lord Mayor took the salute.

There they were – all of them were all right, all fit – and there was I, a crock. As they came back, they were being cheered ... but I was a wreck. I wish I hadn't been there to see it – to see my own battery coming back. I couldn't help it, I always felt bitter. I think that was one of the saddest times of my life.

Charles Carrington

The first Armistice Day had been a carnival. The second Armistice Day, after its solemn pause for the Two-Minutes' Silence which George V was believed to have initiated, was a day of festivity again. For some years I was one of a group of friends who met, every Armistice Day, at the Café Royal for no end of a party, until we found ourselves out of key with the new age. Imperceptibly, the Feast-Day became a Fast Day and one could hardly go brawling on the Sabbath. The do-gooders captured the Armistice and the British Legion seemed to make its principal outing a day of mourning. To march to the Cenotaph was too much like attending one's own funeral, and I know many old soldiers who found it increasingly discomforting, year by year. We preferred our reunions in private with no pacifist propaganda.

Field-Marshal Sir Henry Wilson

On 4 October 1920, Dean Ryle (Westminster Abbey) came to see me with a proposal which greatly pleased me. He wants to exhume the body of a private soldier (not identified) in France and bury it with full honours in Westminster Abbey, putting a plain stone over it saying something to the effect 'Here lies the body of an unknown British soldier who died for his King and Country, etc.'

I suggested some other word being used than 'soldier' as then this would cover the Navy and Air Force and he agreed. I told him he must ask the King, who returns from Balmoral on Friday. He suggested 11 November for the day.

Edward Hibbert

The body of the 'Unknown Warrior' was chosen from four brought to British Army Head Quarters in Calais, from the battlefields of the Marne, Arras, Cambrai and the Ypres Salient. It was enclosed in a casket of English oak and put aboard the destroyer HMS *Verdun*. The body was wrapped in Padre Railton's Union Jack – a tattered flag which had been on many battlefields, and in solemn ceremony, in Westminster Abbey, the Unknown Warrior was reburied in a hundred bags of French soil from the Ypres battlefield.

Brigadier-General L J Wyatt

GOC British Troops, France and Flanders, 1920 and Director of the War Graves Commission

(letter to the Editor of the *Daily Telegraph*, November 1939)

Sir,

From time to time accounts have been published purporting to relate how and by whom the Unknown Warrior's body was selected in France for burial in Westminster Abbey on Nov 11, 19 years ago. I should like to give here the authentic account of what took place.

In October I received a notification from the War Office that King George V had approved the suggestion and the proposal that the burial should be in Westminster Abbey on Nov 11. I issued instructions that the body of a British soldier, which it would be impossible to identify, should be brought in from each of the four battle areas – the Aisne, the Somme, Arras and Ypres, on the night of Nov 7, and placed in the chapel of St Pol. The party bringing each body was to return at once to its area so that there should be no chance of knowing on which the choice fell.

Reporting to my headquarters office at St Pol, at midnight on Nov 7, Colonel Gell, one of my staff, announced that the bodies were in the chapel, and the men who had brought them had gone. The four bodies lay on stretchers, each covered by a Union Jack; in front of the altar was the shell of the coffin which had been sent from England to receive the remains. I selected one, and with the assistance of Colonel Gell, placed it in the shell. We screwed down the lid. The other bodies were removed and reburied in the military cemetery outside my headquarters at St Pol.

I had no idea even of the area from which the body I selected had come; no-one else can know it ... The shell, under escort was sent to Boulogne ... The next morning, carried by the pall-bearers who were selected from NCOs of the British and Dominion troops, it was placed on a French military wagon and taken to Boulogne Quay, where a British destroyer was waiting ... Six barrels of earth from the Ypres Salient were put on board, to be placed in the tomb at Westminster Abbey, so that the body should rest in the soil on which so many of our troops gave up their lives.

Then HMS *Verdun* moved off, a guard of honour of Bluejackets at 'the Present', carrying that symbol which for so many years, and especially during the last few months, has meant so much to us all.

Herbert Thompson
Veteran blinded in gas attack, one of three representing St Dustan's home for the blind at the inauguration of the tomb of the Unknown Warrior in 1920

The ceremony at the Abbey left an indelible impression on my mind – a feeling of ineffable sadness and melancholy, yet there was a message of inspiration and hope. I felt as if the spirit of the Unknown Soldier had whispered in my ear, 'Courage brother; hope on.' I understood all, even though every step and every movement had to be explained to me by an accompanying guide. The atmosphere was impregnated with meaning. The Great Alchemist by some miracle vouchsafed to me a more powerful vision than those who had eyes to see. Clear-cut pictures of France and Flanders rose up before me. The dread solemnity of the occasion stirred the most poignant memories. I felt with my comrades almost ashamed that I had given so little, while he who was sleeping by us had given all ... I came to the Abbey glad that I had been chosen from among so many. I went away sorrowing, but with the message of hope locked in my heart.

Philip Gibbs, reporting in *The Daily Chronicle* of 12 November

It did not seem an Unknown Warrior whose body came on a gun-carriage down Whitehall where we were waiting for him. He was known to us all. It was one of 'our boys' – not warriors – as we called them in the days of darkness lit by faith ... To some women, weeping a little in the crowd after an all-night vigil, he was their own boy who went missing one day and was never found till now ... To many men wearing ribbons and badges on civil clothes, he was a familiar figure, one of their comrades.

It was the steel helmet – the old 'tin hat' – lying there on the crimson of the flag, which revealed him instantly, not as a mythical warrior, aloof from common humanity, a shadowy type of national pride and martial glory, but as one of those fellows dressed in the drab of khaki, stained by mud and grease, who went into the dirty ditches with this steel hat on his head.

Sergeant W J Collins
Royal Army Medical Corps

They were a wonderful generation ... let's face it, there were we, at the beginning of the war, the regular soldier, tough hardened from India and South Africa, and then the 1st Army, Kitchener's ... grand men they were. I watched a battalion of them march into battle on the Somme in 1916, and I thought to myself, 'My God! What a wonderful lot of chaps.' Fine physically, good, well set up, good marching ... it was a fine generation. It's a great pity it was decimated.

Corporal Tommy Keele

11th Battalion, Middlesex Regiment; attached to 'Ace of Spades' Concert Party

The war changed me in two or three ways. It made me more aggressive and more short-tempered. And I had a thing about butcher shops – that lasted a long time. I couldn't see those bits of meat hanging up because I remembered all the times that I had to bury bits of meat which had been my own comrades. All that made me bad tempered – and one or two other things made me not the bloke that I was before. As a kid I used to love whistling, but after my experiences in the trenches I couldn't whistle. I have never been able to whistle since the war.

I don't think the war changed me in any positive way – I just dropped in with the concert party and that was how I met my girlfriend. I never worried too much about girls during the war. I went to one or two bad houses, but I was never mad about it. Maybe I was getting more aware of sex when I was getting demobbed. It wasn't until I was married that I realized that that bloody war had killed off a lot of my sense of humour and my good nature. I was bad-tempered and my poor wife suffered for it. I would go days without speaking – all this stemmed from the war, but thank God it's over now. I still can't whistle – but I can see the funny side of it.

I don't think it was a war worth fighting. I have often tried to analyse it. It's not that I love the Germans – I still don't – but I hated the Germans in those days. I can't say I have *hated* them ever since, but I've never liked them. The powers that be – the top brass – knew nothing about how to fight a war. The generals wanted to put 10,000 men in this sector, another 10,000 men in that sector – never worrying about whether the sector was safe for those 10,000 men to enter. It would turn out that it wasn't, because by the next day half the 10,000 were dead. I can't think of any general who did anything substantial towards winning that war. They didn't. They went on, sending men in until the Americans came over – which altered the balance of the troops fighting the Germans. The thousands of Americans that came over turned the tide and the Germans just had to give in. I don't look back to our leaders with great affection for having won the war – they didn't. I didn't think about it at the time – I thought what they were doing was the natural thing and it was only afterwards that I reached the conclusion that they had no idea what they were doing. I had nothing against my own senior officers – I loved my colonel, I loved my second-in-command – that's why I became his batman. I can't say I disliked any of them, they were only just slightly superior to me, as I thought at that time – but of course they weren't. I could have been one of them if I wanted – but I didn't want to be commissioned and die the next day. They asked me several times if I would go for a commission and I always had the same answer, 'I will go for a commission if you can guarantee that when I am commissioned I can go into the Royal Flying Corps.' They said they couldn't guarantee it, and it would depend on how I passed out at the school where I was commissioned. If they thought I was material for the Royal Flying Corps they would do that, but if I was material only fit for the trenches, that's what I would be. So I said, 'I am sorry. I won't take a commission. I would sooner be a live lance corporal than a dead officer'. I always wanted to fly . . .

I rather liked the colonials who were fighting with us. The Aussies? I thought they were super people – you couldn't muck them about like you could a British Tommy. If we wanted something we could whistle for it – but if the Australians wanted something you'd got to get it for them, or else. On one occasion we were out of the line, at rest. The officers were housed in a big mansion and the electric light and utilities were all laid on by Australian troops. Some of these Australians went to the officer's mess and said 'Sir, could we have a bottle of whisky?' They said, 'No of course not – whisky doesn't go to other ranks'. They said,

'Sorry sir, we've got a feeling the electric light is a bit on the blink.' They went away and switched the whole bloody lot off – and of course the officers had got no bloody lights. The Aussies went back and said, 'Sorry about the lights – but that bottle of whisky would have helped.' They got a bottle of whisky. We couldn't do that, not the British troops – but the Aussies could.

Corporal Charles Templar
13th Battalion, Gloucestershire Regiment

I am certain that my experience of the war made a great deal of difference to my outlook on life. Once you have been shot at and in very great danger of being killed on more than one occasion, life becomes very precious to you. I wouldn't have missed those experiences for the world – given that I had survived. Moreover, I am sure that it had a great deal of influence on my married life. Daisy and I were very grateful for the fact that I had survived and that was very important. All our married life she wanted to be involved with anything that I was doing – we worked together to build the business – we worked together in everything and there were never any secrets between us. There was a feeling of joy and gratitude in the fact that I had survived, which made it possible for us to enjoy our married life together. I think it did me a lot of good. It made me realize that what I had got to do was to provide. It was no good sitting and waiting for somebody else to do something for me – I had to get up and do it myself.

Corporal Clifford Lane
2nd Battalion, Bedford and Hertfordshire Regiment

The war taught me a lot about human nature – and I learnt about myself too. I found that I had sufficient endurance to last out through cold and wet and harsh conditions. I nearly got pneumonia once, but I got through it. I must have had a strong constitution to have survived it. We were nervously exhausted after the war for quite a time, all we wanted to do was lead a quiet life.

I never got any sort of pension – I never applied for one, although I could have. I know that afterwards quite a lot of people got pensions for what was essentially nervous exhaustion. I think I could have got a pension for that. You had to apply within seven years. I know people who got pensions for bronchitis – people who never left England, but still got a pension for life.

Looking back I'd take it as a truism, that the only people that really experienced the war in all its horror were the frontline infantry. No question about that at all. That's why they were called the PBI – the Poor Bloody Infantry. It was fully justified; I've got no doubt about that. People in the battalion headquarters didn't go over the top – in fact, people at brigade headquarters didn't really know much about it. Compared with us, people in divisional HQ were living the life of Riley. People who were on these big guns were miles behind the line – they were never at the frontline. The first people to attend to the wounded would be your own stretcher-bearers. Indeed, you were lucky to get any attention. When you got to the RAMC, you were getting out, away out of the danger zone. You knew that you were in one place and the enemy were about thirty or forty yards away – and there is nothing between you. You never knew what you were going to encounter when you were on patrol. You would go sixty yards out and you would stay there – you'd got to remember you had nobody in front of you except the enemy, who might attack at any time.

Ruby Ord
Women's Army Auxiliary Corps

By the way we were trained, they were trying to make troops of us, which I always resented. I didn't join an 'army' – I always want to be a woman, and I didn't want to be imitating the men. I wanted the status of women to be established in their own right. I didn't want women to be given 'equality' with men, because I've always felt we are a bit superior, so that stance always shocked me. Men used to look up to women – and you don't look up to your equal. All the same, it was quite a good life.

My experiences in the war definitely changed me. It was such an unusual experience for our day to go away from home and to be with so many people – living always among a crowd. No doubt it was very good for us, and I must say they were a fine lot of women – but they were specially picked in the first place. But they were brave enough to volunteer. They hadn't the faintest idea what it would be like. Some of them did not stay the course and they were sent home – but most of them showed all sorts of courage in raids. On one occasion we were in a hotel and there was a woman who was a motor transport driver and very, very good at her job. A raid started and all the staff of the hotel went down to the basement – and they told us we could do so too, but we didn't. You were in the dark immediately in that war when there was a raid and everything was just switched off at the mains, so you had no light. We had two officers there who were suffering from shellshock and the men with them were in a panic, so one of our girls felt her way over to the piano and played for two hours while the raid lasted. We all sang and these shell-shocked officers didn't seem to know there was a raid on. Afterwards the men were overwhelmed at her courage and staying power, and they said, 'If anybody ever says a bad word about the WAACS they'll have to answer to us for it after this.'

People were very ready to criticize us, especially when we came home on leave – we were the women who had followed the men to France. There were several incidents where the girls showed outstanding courage, and I thought they were remarkable. They were so adaptable, so capable. No situation ever arose where they couldn't do what was required of them. I am a great admirer of my own sex.

Perhaps the good Lord provided women who could fit the bill through two world wars, because they were mums in the Second World War or grandmas. They had to look after children and there are a remarkable number of women in my generation whom I admire tremendously for so many reasons.

The women's role in the war was very important. They had no training and whatever they went to do, they were turned to as a last resort – so they weren't prepared. But they did the job – and they did it awfully well. It blew a gaffe that men were the superior sex, even at work and in munitions factories. Everywhere women went, they did wonderfully well – but I don't think that it was a good thing for their home life. That is my only regret – it drew women away from their homes and I think the country deteriorated in consequence. But women set the standards, not just morally but in every way. I think the strength of the nation is in the home and when the home weakens, the nation does too.

These days I am a pacifist, so if my time came again I wouldn't do the same thing. I would say 'no, let us be strong – all of us – and refuse to fight'. It is the only way to end war.

Sergeant Harry Hopthrow
Royal Engineers

There was a strange gulf between those who had been to the war and those who had not – and that lasted for many years. There was always a feeling that they were two distinct groups of people and that the military people were disparaging about those who hadn't been. This was noticeable for many years after the war. I often heard quite senior people in my company apologizing for not having been in the war – although they had probably worked manufacturing explosives, which I would have thought was a more dangerous job.

Quite a lot of men decided they'd had enough of soldiering when the war ended. I sometimes wondered how serious it was, whether they were what one might call 'inverted hypocrites', but I was never able to assess whether that was so or not. One came across enormous differences, I knew one young man who was working in the same office as I was when I got back, and he had lost his leg in the war. He had joined quite late, probably under conscription, had been sent to France and was going up the line and within minutes of getting within range of the enemy, he lost his leg. That was his experience of war and he was brought back. He was a most enthusiastic soldier; he regretted intensely that he had missed it all. On the other hand you got people who felt quite the opposite, whether they were wounded or not.

Captain Charles Gee
9th Battalion, Durham Light Infantry

I think I grew up a lot through my experience of the war. I am thinking particularly of something that happened after I was awarded the Military Cross. I was on leave, walking around Newcastle with a friend, and I was wearing my MC, and I remember saying to him, 'I don't feel I deserve this.' To which he replied, 'Oh, don't worry. You've been out there a long time and done a lot of good work.' But I had never done any actual fighting. It was only recently that I realized that I HAD done a lot of very good work, particularly when we were based near Rheims – that had been ten days' super work. Things like getting all the transport in the right place – along with all the water carts and ensuring that there was water to fill the men's water bottles. All the grenades had to be fused, and I had to do that in the dark. I got transport up in the wood and made sure that everything was in the right place. It kept me very busy, making sure everything ran properly. Someone described to me the route to go back to the transport line, 'You go up this road until you get to the three dead mules – and then you turn right and another right. You go on until you see the six dead men.' That was just the practicalities of it. I had not been trained for any of that stuff, but I just did it automatically. It made me consider whether I deserved it as much as most people or less.

Private Joseph Pickard
1/5th Battalion, Northumberland Fusiliers

It's hard to say what I got out of my experience of the war. Maybe I got a certain amount of satisfaction – I was determined to go and I am glad I went. I've never complained about being in the war. It made me a man. By the time I was fifteen and a half, I was standing on my feet – when you're among men, you had to stand up for yourself. I had my fights when I was fifteen. I got so that I didn't give a hoot who was speaking to me and who wasn't. I have always said that I've never regretted anything in my life except the death of my wife. I've had thirty-three operations – right up to just recently.

I was awarded a pension from the army, but as soon as possible I got a job and I had a wage coming in, so I don't suppose it affected me that much. My wife got all my wages, and I lived on my pension, which paid for backing horses, playing cards. I didn't do so badly over the years – I was pretty satisfied.

Sergeant William Cowley
Army Service Corps

Looking back on the war I'd say it was a positive experience – it made me more responsible. It was marvellous – I felt I could do any job. In fact, when I went back to my old job, I got in touch with the Ministry of Labour and they used to send me details of jobs for me to consider, all over the country – but they weren't suitable for me. However, one day they asked if I'd go to Coventry to see some major with a view to opening a labour exchange. I didn't know whether I could ask for the time off, because I had a regimental sergeant major for a boss – so I never went. But I know I could have done it.

Nora Baker
Women's Army Auxiliary Corps, who worked as gardener in Abbeville and Wimereux war cemeteries

Once I was demobbed I came home, and I for one didn't think anything about it. Then they formed what they called the Dinner Club which held a big gathering in London at Derry and Tom's once a year and I used to go up to that from Grantham. There were hundreds and hundreds of us.

I've never returned to look at the graves – I've met people who have been out there, but I somehow have no wish to.

The war certainly gave women opportunities they wouldn't ordinarily have had – but I was a very ordinary person – nondescript – and I don't think it particularly changed me. I don't feel it gave me any greater sense of independence or equality with men. Once I was home, I just fell into the normal routine – my husband was a wealthy man as regards his job. He had a wealthy business in Grantham. He had a very rich old father who put him and his brother into the business.

All the same, now if there's anything to do with the Commonwealth War Graves you will find me there. I go up to London for the Armistice Day service and I get an invitation to stand with all the big noises. I look forward to that very much, but I have given away all my belongings from the war.

Private William Holmes
12th Battalion, London Regiment

I always look back on the war as an experience. I had just as much pleasure out of the good times as I did the bad times. True, I saw some horrific scenes and the bombardments when men were going over and being blown to bits. But the point was that we were so disciplined that we took it all for granted – almost as if it was normal.

I don't honestly think it changed my character – I never felt any different afterwards – but I always remember all those mates of mine in the trenches. We were just a band of brothers. No brothers could have been more united than we were. No-one ever knew if they were going to be dead the next minute – but that's how we lived. I remember them – but I didn't stay in touch.

Guardsman Frederick 'Fen' Noakes

The people welcomed us, not as conquerors, but as deliverers from war. That was the universal feeling – relief that the war was over, at any price. Also, our presence was a safeguard against the time of revolution, which was rampant in the rest of Germany. And our men, by their correct behaviour and lack of 'Prussian' swagger, soon became genuinely popular.

During that Christmas-tide of 1918, I think that, had matters been left to the soldiers and the common people, such a peace of reconciliation and mutual good-will could have been made which would not only have fulfilled the ideals for which millions had died, but would have secured a lasting friendship between the erstwhile enemies. The men who had fought and suffered, on both sides, had had their fill of war, and were ready for a peace based on Christian concord without malice. But the soldiers were virtually disenfranchized, the politicians took control and imposed a vindictive treaty the like of which was never seen in the modern world before. All our subsequent troubles and frustrations date from that – the supreme opportunity was thrown away.

Gunner William Towers
Royal Field Artillery

Of course the war wasn't worth it – God no! It was a waste of time. If men had been sensible it would never have happened. I realized what a waste it was. What the devil were they doing, killing fellows that had nothing to do with it? We had nothing to do with it – it was all to do with them in Parliament. Instead, they ought to let them have a battle between them. Why not let *them* go and fight one another until they made it better?

We needn't have got involved, and the way it was, you lost your patriotism. It was so stupid – that was the thing. I realized it was stupid. It didn't give me any political attitude, but I always felt a resentment – and I was just glad it was over.

Lieutenant Richard Dixon
Royal Garrison Artillery
(writing 50 years later)

I think we saw quite clearly enough what we were doing, and that we had a filthy job on hand that had to be done. But I can testify to our feelings by 1918, and these feelings were practically universal among the fighting troops, and commonly expressed. We were quite sure we were going to win the war, but, we said, 'the politicians will lose it for us afterwards'.

And at Versailles, sure enough they did ... The Treaty of Versailles contained within its provisions the seeds of the next conflict, which made it inevitable.

Frank Gillard

Nothing was worth it. Why is any of it worth it? Just because a few politicians fall out over power and a bit of land they gain and they use the people on that bit of land as pawns. Worthwhile? No! Why was it worthwhile? The only worthwhile part was that we prevented the Germans from coming and taking our country. Then you came home and everything was ruined. We were rationed and you couldn't buy anything. I was out of work and that was that. I expect it turned me politically – I became a socialist. I certainly thought that political power was wrong, and the country and the world were being run by people that had not got the wherewithal.

Corporal Hawtin Mundy
5th Battalion, Oxfordshire and Buckinghamshire Light Infantry

What's this country today? When they held their heads high with pride, Great Britain ruled the world – the sun never set on the British Empire. They were days of pride – that's what you fought for. Today it's all been given away. What's left? Nothing. Don't you think those chaps that lived in those days would look round and say, 'Cor blimey, what did we fight for?'

I was three times wounded, and twenty months a prisoner of

war – so I can speak from experience and give my view of what the war was and why I didn't think there were such things as heroes or cowards. Now, I weighed it all up, and my view of heroes was the millions that lined up outside recruiting offices – that's my view of heroes. Now years and years later, when we have got old, my old darling and I went to the Albert Hall on the 11th November for the British Legion Remembrance service. At the end of that service, the lights were dimmed, the poppies slowly fell down from the roof, the buglers sounded the Last Post, and then a loud, clear voice said, 'At the going down of the sun and in the morning, we will remember them.'

Sergeant Ernest Woodward

In the first few years after the war, hollow words were used too often at the unveiling of war memorials. Glib words about the 'Great Sacrifice'. I know that in many cases these words were used with deep feeling by men who had lost their own sons. They became almost a cliché in the oratory of politicians. Laurence Binyon's noble words 'they shall not grow old as we who are left grow old' took on an ironic meaning in the mouths of speakers who were well content to grow old and fat, and who had never asked the dead whether they had chosen to die young in order to avoid old age. As time went on, I began to dislike more and more the celebration of Armistice Day. I wished that all the formal ceremonies might be abandoned, and that this commemoration of the dead could be left to those for whom it had some personal meaning. Darkness is not better than light, death is not better than life; no praise from comfortable men can bring the dead back to the sun they loved. It was too easy for the older generation to find a convenient anodyne in the formal politeness of a two-minutes' silence, in the weaving of wreaths, in the provision of adequate pensions for widows and orphans.

Private Leonard Davies
Royal Air Force

I don't think I felt any long-lasting effects after the war. I always thank God that I got through it as I did – and so did my parents. It's quite remarkable, because I don't feel I did anything of any particular importance, and yet I went right through all that hardship in the Army and the air force, and I have been very healthy ever since. I think my present health is due entirely to my wife, who has always looked after me – fed me properly. We've been married fifty years.

I don't think the war affected me, except one thing that I have always regretted – and that's that I wasn't able to finish my course in aerodynamics and mechanical engineering at the polytechnic. I got an honours diploma when I left the polytechnic in 1914. I came out of that war and there were absolutely no jobs going in aerodynamics at all – no work on aeroplanes. We had reached our peak and we weren't doing anymore. It was all very disappointing.

Looking back, what I do know is that that type of fighting will never fix anything – it will only bring more trouble. There's no question about that. You beat a man down, but it doesn't mean to say you've got him to agree to do anything at all. We beat the Germans by brutality, by sheer force – and that can't do anybody any good. It never does. You have got to talk to people – convince them in some way. But I believe that using force can never bring things to a satisfactory conclusion.

Now I wouldn't fight another war – I would absolutely refuse. I wouldn't have anything to do with it. I would do all I could to promote a peaceful conclusion. I think good comes out of every war, because good things do happen – and intensely brave people emerge. I am sure there is a lot of goodness to come out of the war, if someone can identify it – but I couldn't spot it.

Private Harry Wells
23rd Battalion, Royal Fusiliers

I think there's renewed interest now in the First World War. It was a terrible catastrophe – such heavy losses. At the time, the people at home didn't dream of what was happening. The true horror was kept away from the people, but now they are able to release what really happened in the First World War. It was so dreadful – 20,000 men annihilated in one day on the Somme – it's hard to imagine. These days when we go to the memorial gatherings and commemorations, it's amazing to see how many civilians come along.

In a way, although it's not something they would have wanted to be involved in, the young people today seem to have missed something in their lifetime. Every generation had a war.

Private K Hares
Oxfordshire and Buckinghamshire Light Infantry

War is so futile. There is no end to it – no finality. These days, if anything comes on the goggle box to do with war I switch it off. At the time, I felt I wouldn't be there long – but it was just the luck of the war. You are too concerned with your own safety and immediate environment and your pals around you. You do as you are told and you don't ask questions – you are not told why you have to do it. You are told to march through the forest at night – you are told to fall out on the side of the road – you are told to rest and you are lucky, because you've found a pile of stones to sleep on. You come out on a rest, and everybody else has fixed themselves up with billets so you are left with the pigsty. That happened to me. You fall into a cesspool, you delouse yourself. As I have said it is bloody marvellous if you can come through that. I met a chap, older than me, and he went right through the war and all the events on the Western Front and he didn't have a blooming scratch on him.

Sapper George Clayton
175 Tunnelling Company, Royal Engineers

The only way I can look at the whole experience of war was that it was the height of madness. I have seen it, and I couldn't describe it in any other way. I remember once, just after the battle at Messines, I volunteered with a party of men to go out and carry the wounded away – but the dead were lying everywhere. It was an awful job. I wouldn't go for another war.

I can't say I have any regrets about that war. You never knew if you were going to get out of the trench alive because while there was everything to protect you, there was everything to destroy you, too. There was warfare in the air, warfare on the ground and warfare underground. I was underground in the tunnels, and in some ways it was a happy-go-lucky existence when you were there – but still I wouldn't volunteer again.

Ruby Ord
Women's Army Auxiliary Corps

Looking back, the hardships and suffering weren't worthwhile – they never are. War doesn't achieve anything that's worthwhile. I hadn't been demobilized long before I became a pacifist and found myself sympathizing with people who had the courage to refuse to fight – because they are the only people who will ever end war. I think women could have done this. Now with nuclear war, I don't know what we could do.

Before the war I despised the pacifists – although I don't think I would have given out a white feather, because I wouldn't know if maybe a man had an illness or some good reason for not joining up. However, I would still have despised people who were unwilling to fight. In fact, I used to go and speak about it at meetings – I was so crazy. That is why I think my reaction is genuine, because I am a thinker – I do not react emotionally. But when I go to reunions, when I have to toast the forces, I feel fed up with it. I do it, just to be amiable and not upset the applecart, because one of the women sitting there's got two sons in the Navy – but they know my feelings. I didn't ever want to wear a uniform. I went out as a woman, to help. They wanted women to help to release men for the forces and that was all I did. I was fantastically patriotic. This is something that's died in the country, it's all 'me and never mind the country', now.

Private Ernest Lye
Duke of Wellington's Regiment

If every man who fought in the Great War was to take up a pen and put his impressions on paper, we should get no two stories alike, yet I venture to predict that one and all who saw the hideousness and horror and walked hand in hand with Death for months at a time, would be in agreement that nothing whatever can justify WAR. If we who have tasted war's bitter cup could impress that upon the coming generation, our sacrifices will not have been in vain.

Lance-Corporal William Sharpe

Memories of the late war MUST never fade. Let everything about it be known. Teach it to our children: make it lurid, emphasize it, preach it, *glorify* it as the Biggest and Best Argument for Peace evermore.

Sergeant Stewart Jordan

1/14th Battalion, London Regiment

When I got back, I suppose I was a bit older. I've got two photographs – one showing me when I first joined up, and one after four years of war. I had lost a bit of hair and was a bit thinner I think, but thankfully I kept remarkably well. I don't think the war had any lasting mental effects. I did think that what I had done was worthwhile. I felt I had done my bit – done what I could. We all felt that we had to do something to prevent the Germans getting over here: which we did. I think we were all very relieved that it was over and that I had come through it safely.

Annie May Martin

Women's Army Auxiliary Corps

At one stage when the war was going so very badly, they did contemplate sending all the women home, but the GOC at the base said that if the signals went, communications would collapse, because they were all staffed by women – and this released hundreds of men to go up to the Front. The contribution of women at home was immense too. It was a very big factor, because women had done so much in the war, on equal terms with the men. The experience of being in the war made the women a little more demanding and more sure of themselves. I would say, in the post war years, that the hardships and sacrifice had been worthwhile.

Private James Hewitt

7th Battalion, Leicestershire Regiment

Looking back, I'd say that in some instances the hardships and sacrifices of the war were not worthwhile – but circumstances alter in each individual case. I would say I have no regrets and I think that it was worthwhile overall. Whether the politicians think it was, I don't know, but I'd say on the basis of what we went for, yes, it was worthwhile.

There were conscientious objectors, and I didn't mind them at all – a good many of them served just as well as any man in the line, by dint of the humanitarian work they did. Often they went out under fire to bring a wounded man in. They were as good as any other man and they did more for humanity than the average man would.

Lord Plumer of Messines

(on the unveiling of the Menin Gate, 1927)

One of the most tragic features of the Great War was the number of casualties reported as 'missing, believed killed'.

To their relatives there must have been added to their grief a tinge of bitterness and a feeling that everything possible had not been done to recover their loved ones' bodies, and give them reverent burial ... when peace came, and the last ray of hope had been extinguished, the void seemed deeper and the outlook more forlorn for those who had no grave to visit, no place where they could lay tokens of loving remembrance ... and it was resolved that here at Ypres, where so many of the missing are known to have fallen, there should be erected a memorial worthy of them which should give expression to the nation's gratitude for their sacrifice and their sympathy with those who mourned them. A memorial has been erected which, in its simple grandeur, fulfils this object, and now it can be said of each one in whose honour we are assembled here today ... 'He is not missing; he is here!'

Corporal Hawtin Mundy
5th Battalion, Oxfordshire and Buckinghamshire Light Infantry

I wrote a message, to place on a grave on the Somme of an old friend of mine that was killed. I wrote, 'Sleep well, comrades. You held your heads high with pride, but now they would bow in shame, as all that is left are memories'.

Corporal Harold Bashford
Bedfordshire and Hertfordshire Regiment

Having left England in December '16 in very severe weather, our return conditions were identical. During my first week home, I went out skating on the same pond where in those lovely summers as a boy I used to fish, hearing the turtle doves and, as the light faded, listening to the twittering of swallows as they came in to roost among the overhanging willows. That to me is still a lovely memory, looking back over my war service and recalling how often death was a possibility. The question as to why I survived, I really don't know. Coming from a Christian background my mother would have prayed for my safe return and hoped her prayers would be answered. But what of the thousands of other mothers whose prayers were unanswered or ignored? It seemed to me prayer and war were incompatible and that it is all a game of chance. If the dice is loaded against you, your chance of survival is very slim indeed.

Upon return, those of us who had been pupils at Saddlescomb Elementary School and had been on active service, received a fraying testimonial beautifully printed in 'Olde English' by our old headmaster, H.W. Martin, headed, 'By the glory of God have I fought men'. I said that, while appreciating this recognition, I could not help feeling that the choice of words was unfortunate. How many, I wonder, found glory in killing or maiming fellow human beings where there was no personal enmity. These sixty-five years since my return I count as a bonus – almost a whole lifetime. It has been a lifetime denied to so many of my pals who failed to return and tell their story. It certainly made me question what it was all about. You just wondered if there wasn't a better way of settling arguments than this.

We didn't hear much of conscientious objectors, pacifists and people who would not fight. I think that they had the courage of their convictions. My sister married a conscientious objector and she didn't despise him for it. He said, 'If they shoot me so be it, but I am not prepared to shoot anyone else, though I have got nothing against those who do fight.' That was what he felt about it. I think there won't be another war – I think it will be a 'press the button' affair and we shall all be gone in a flash. But I am pretty sure that there would have been many more conscientious objectors if the fathers who had lived through the Great War told their sons what it was all about. It would be for them to wonder if they could face it – and I don't think some of them could – I don't know whether we could either, if we had known beforehand how hard it was going to be.

I know I would have found it difficult to put a bayonet in somebody. I thank God I was never engaged in hand-to-hand fighting, because I'm not sure what my reaction to that would have been. I know we were told that if we didn't do it to them, they would do it to us, and that was the only thing that spurred us on – the fact that it was either him or you. But I don't think men should ever be asked to do that sort of thing.

It was getting on for two years after the outbreak of war when I was called up. There was all this enthusiasm and these chaps went into it with a sense of enjoyment that they were going to fight for King and Country. There was that Kitchener saying, 'Your Country needs You'. But that spirit gradually disappeared. You went because you were called up and there was a job – and whatever it was, you'd got to do it. There was never any enthusiasm for it. If it was for King and Country, so be it – but I was never quite sure what it was all about. I don't think men ought to be asked to do it – ever.

Captain Henry Williamson
Bedfordshire Regiment

We reached Ypres in the late afternoon. It is unrecognizable: 'Wipers' exists in the memory only. The city today is clean and new and hybrid-English. Its vast Grande Place holds enough air and sunlight to give a feeling of freedom and space. The rectangular ruined fragment of the Cloth Hall is contained in its scaffold box. Grasses and wild flowers on the tops of the walls make the ruin beautiful. In spring the jackdaws feed their young in the nests within the masonry gaps on high. The less unobservant American visitors notice the four-way trumpets of the siren on the top of the ruin, and ask their guides if it is 'the old original gas-horns of the British'?

Alas, there is no historical thrill about that siren. It is a modern instrument fixed there by the local Fire Brigade. During the daytime the Grande Place is the parking place for motorcars and charabancs. A handbill may be put into your hand by a Belgian, an amusing document with its quaint spelling, 'First class cars for hire. Competition impossible.' 'Carefull (sic) drivers. Highly recommended and very popular with visitors tours to Belgium, the prices quoted as for first class car, including an experienced guide explaining all the places of interest, visited or passed, and are inclusive, absolutely nothing extra.'

Long grasses and wild trees grow on the ramparts. When you

walk there at twilight, wary of the broken tops of the sally-ports, you see the new houses, all without a chip or a tile missing; but they do not obscure the passing of the men. No, it is not men – it is a force that is passing, an invisible wind that hurls down the stones and the bricks soundlessly, that fills the Grande Place and all the street with cries and shouts and the last screams of the dying, and yet all is without sound.

I left the ramparts, and sought the café where my foot-weary companion was awaiting me. There was much noise in there, and the lights were bright. Men were playing billiards, others talked with animation at the tables. Waiters hurried with trays of filled glasses. I heard the click of billiard balls, the happy Saturday night chatter of men who know they need not work on the morrow. Smoke straying from pipes and cigarettes, laughter. 'Good health!' from my friend to me. I looked up, took a pull at the pale yellow beer and nodded to him; but the café scene fades, and I am a wraith again in the darkness rushing by, yet stagnant amid the soundless cries, the viewless white flashes of field guns lighting the broken wall and the scattered rubble; the misery of men marching, laden and sweating, through the ruin of the Menin Gate. Passing strings of men slouching away from the line, thinking only of sleep, sleep, sleep; slouching on, anywhere, anyhow, puttees over boots, feet swelled and unfelt, stumbling, but slouching on again.

I get up and go back to the ramparts. The evening star is a rayless bright point of silver in the western sky. The edges of the moat are dimly whitened with cement rocks tipped from the bank. There are tins too, and rusty lengths of angle-iron. Nettles grow out of the concrete machine-gun shelters on the further bank. Below in a boat pushed into the reeds, an old man is fishing. Everything is normal for him; he is using bread pills to catch the roach which roam in shoals from the Menin to the Lille Gates.

The border of ground under the ramparts is sown with dwarf beans and potatoes. It is his allotment – he has finished weeding for the evening and is enjoying a pipe and the watching of his float. He sees only reed, water, lilies, his quill float, and the peaceful summer sky above the green field. He hears only the sirens of motorcars, and the loud confident song-chatter of the reed-warblers in the reeds.

Outside the hotel, beside the laid-out flower gardens, are two howitzers and a shattered British tank. An American came up while I was trying the rusty elevating gear of one how, and asked me what it was. I told him it had fired 9-inch shells on Ypres from Houthulst Forest. 'There's a better specimen over there,' I said, pointing to the other fifty yards away. 'This one will do,' he replied. 'Now I've only got to see Hill 60, the holes at Messines, the Bloodchapel at Bruges, and the Death Trench, then I'm through.' He hurried away.

Hill 60 is one of the show-places of the Salient today. Every morning about a dozen peasants go there to dig. You see the 'souvenirs' they have dug up lying on sacks or lengths of cloth at the edge of the pits in which they are working. There are wooden pipes, both British and German shape, well preserved in the light sandy soil, fragments of rifles, bayonets, pickelhaube eagle-badges, English county and London regimental badges, buttons, traps, bully beef tins, pistols, bombs, revolvers, boots. Imagine an ant-hill fifty yards across its base, thrown up a few dozen times by subterranean heavings, and dropping again after each mine-explosion more or less in the same place; always being pocked and repocked with shells; and now set with a small memorial to the 9th London Regiment, and dug over, and strolled over by 10,000 every week.

All day long, charabancs stop in the road opposite Hill 60, and tourists file past the melancholy little group of men and children standing, collecting box in hand, by the footpath entrance and hoping to take half a franc off each visitor. By their sad faces they do not own the heap of earth, originally piled there when the railway cutting was made; yet by the occasional gleams of hate in those eyes, we deduce that they have stood there with their box long enough to believe that they ought to own it.

I remember a solitary grave standing in the middle of a grassy valley in this country of rolling gentle downland; a grave that we came upon with a strange wonder and silence, set with a blade of a propeller for headstone, with pansies and mignonette and violets for coverlet, railed off from the cattle around the resting place of the 'brave, unknown English airman who fell in battle, July 14, 1916'. Today, more than ten years afterwards, I stand and watch the German graves in one of those remembered places being dug up, and brown bones and scraps of rag being shovelled into boxes, roughly in the shape of coffins, but very narrow. The tall blond Flemish labourers pick up the fragments and toss them in. What remains of the grey uniform cloth is black and brittle as old mushroom fragments dried by the sun.

An Englishman supervises with a French gendarme. The Englishman stands there to see that no English bones are taken in mistake, for in wartime, friend and foe were often buried together. But not in peace-time – that time when nations (or those minding the business of other people) practise war and invent new ways of death. The bones of the slain may lie side by side at peace in wartime, but in peace-time they are religiously separated into nations again, each to its place – the British to the white gardens 'that are forever England', and the others to the German cemetery – the Labyrinth.

THE LAST SURVIVORS

Shortly before the completion of this book, more than ninety years after the Armistice, the last two British veterans of the Great War died. They alone could give first-hand testimony of the conflict – an experience which had informed their lives,

*and which remained the cornerstone of their outlook on life,
and their sense of the preciousness of every minute.*

Henry Allingham
Born 6 June 1896, served in the Royal Flying Corps

People still talk a lot of rubbish about the war. I've always let
people know what really went on. I suppose I was breaking the
rules. I've let people know so that the truth could be a warning
to them. When the war was going on, its horrors were kept quiet
and the full display of dreadful things only came out afterwards.
These things were carefully hidden at the time. There was wartime
censorship and the most gruesome things were concealed. These
days, if any trigger-happy politician wants to start another war,
it's my job to let people know what that means. Politicians today
are pitiless humbugs. What do they know? Only those who were
there can tell what really happened. Tell of the suffering and
misery.

Harry Patch
Born 17 June 1898, served with the Duke of Cornwall's Light Infantry

Even ninety-two years afterwards, I still remember. I still com-
memorate 22 September and remember the three friends I lost on
Pilckem Ridge. They are always with me. I don't do anything.
I don't feel like talking. I've always remembered it. I don't join in
when people sing all the old songs, and I don't watch war films.
Why should I? I was there. I can see that damned explosion
now.

Why should the British Government call me up and take me
out to a battlefield to shoot a man I never knew, whose language

I couldn't speak? All those lives lost for a war finished over a table. Now what is the sense in that? It's just an argument between two governments. I never want any other man to go through what we did again – but still we send our lads to war, being killed and being told to kill.

I don't think it is possible to truly explain the bond that is forged between a soldier in the trenches and his fellow soldiers. There you all are, no matter what your life was in Civvy Street, covered in lice, desperately hungry, eking out the small treats – the ounce of tobacco, the biscuit. You relied on him and he on you, never really thinking that it was just the same for the enemy – but it was. It was every bit as bad.

Bibliography

Published works:

Crozier, Brigadier-General F. P., *A Brass Hat in No-Man's Land* (Jonathan Cape, 1930)

Gregory, Adrian, *Silence of Memory* (Berg Publishers, 1994)

Macdonald, Lyn, *Ordeal By Fire* (Folio Society, 2001)

Macdonald, Lyn, *Voices and Images of the Great War* (Penguin, 1991)

Middlebrooke, Martin, *First Day on the Somme* (Norton & Co, ✓ 1972)

Nicholson, Virginia, *Singled Out* (Penguin, 2007)

Williamson, Henry, *The Wet Flanders Plain* (Faber and Faber, 1929)

Woodward E. L., *Short Journey* (Faber and Faber, 1952)

Websites:
Days of Pride
Aftermath

Archives:
Imperial War Museum
Liddle Archive

Index